Seal Secrets:
Cornwall and the Isles of Scilly

Sue Sayer

Pocket Cornwall

TOR MARK

Alison Hodge is an imprint of Tor Mark Ltd,
United Downs Industrial Estate, St Day,
Redruth, Cornwall TR16 5HY

Published 2023

www.tormark.co.uk

ISBN 9780 85025 802 8

Printed and bound in the UK

 Printed on FSC Mix

CONTENTS

'Upside-down V plane'

INTRODUCTION

Cornwall's most reliably sighted, predictable and iconic marine mammal, grey seals are creatures whose lives connect our terrestrial world to the sea. The margin between land and sea is exposed to the rawest and toughest conditions in nature – welcome to the world of the grey seal! They are one of the rarest seal species on our planet, yet common around the coasts of Cornwall and the Isles of Scilly.

Grey seals are both powerful and stunningly beautiful. Their glistening bodies are resilient, yet flexibly sleek as they dance through the white water of our most awesome of winter breakers. In a quieter, reflective moment, I sit on a cliff top on a calm sunny day. Suddenly I am joined by a seal in the glimmering sea. The inquisitive nature of a grey seal becomes apparent as it glances up curiously, making eye contact with me, before exhaling and diving effortlessly out of sight.

I cannot remember when I first saw a grey seal, nor when I fell in love with them. I have since developed a passion that has become an inspiring focus in my life. I would have seen grey seals during my annual Scottish holidays as a child, but it was my first pair of binoculars that transformed my passing interest into an enthusiastic obsession! In this magnified circular world, I saw seals emerge from the sea for the first time. I was rewarded with zoomed in views of seals going about their daily lives, almost as if I was among them. I was hooked. I hope to share some of their secrets with you!

ABOUT THIS BOOK

Photos of cute white coated seal pups hide the harsh realities of their lives. This book provides a glimpse at the hidden and secret world of Cornwall's grey seals from cradle to grave.

'Seal Secrets' has been written from the perspective of an observational researcher, who has spent far too many hours watching and recording seals in the wild in Cornwall, the Isles of Scilly and beyond. It is hoped that this book will provide a unique insight into the private and often surprising lives of our grey seals and includes true stories about real individual wild seals.

Anthropomorphising used to be discouraged by the scientific community. Close observation of seals shows their ongoing communication. As with human mammals, much of this is non-verbal body language. Seals can communicate over 10s of metres to evoke another's response. Science has begun to describe basic personality traits of seals, but we still have a long way to go to understand the complex world of what it is like to be a seal.

Italics have been used when telling the individual stories of real wild seals.

This book begins to describe seal behaviour to create vibrant images for the reader. When watching seals, my aim is to try and understand the motivation behind their hugely varied behaviour and interactions. To eliminate such descriptions greatly diminishes the richness of the social interactivity of this highly developed and intelligent marine creature.

Sue with Cornwall Seal Group Research Trust's (CSGRT) Steering Group

Mum 'Tiny heart' and her pup

ABOUT THE AUTHOR'S RESEARCH

When I started trying to recognise individual seals, I would sit on the cliff top, drawing their fur patterns seen through my binoculars. This was a painstaking process, but a good way to imprint the fur patterns in my brain.

The invention of digital photography and 8 gigabyte SD memory cards was revolutionary, making the capture of hundreds of photographs of an individual seal from all different angles possible and affordable.

I have spent thousands of hours at exposed sites, literally in all weathers observing seals, always at a distance. Observation must be remote for seal behaviour to be natural and unmodified by my presence.

All the photographs in this book have been taken from cliff tops. Originally this was by digiscoping (using a compact camera attached to a telescope), enabling magnifications rarely achievable through affordable SLR cameras.

Nowadays I use a superzoom bridge camera capable of 125× optical magnification and 64 gigabyte SD cards, which is frankly mind-blowing.

For more information about my work, please visit: www.cornwallsealgroup.co.uk or email: sightings@cornwallsealgroup.co.uk/ seals@cornwallsealgroup.co.uk

Acknowledgements

Many thanks to:-
My fellow trustees, many friends in Cornwall Seal Group Research Trust (CSGRT) and all our partner organisations who are a constant source of inspiration, encouragement and support.

A large network of awesome CSGRT community-based volunteers monitoring, representing and looking after seals on their local patch without whom the findings in this book would have been greatly diminished.

James Barnett for proofreading the original manuscript and checking my draft for factual accuracy.

My partner for his unfailing patience and tolerance. He has given me the freedom to follow my life's passion and obsession with grey seals.

CSGRT research is always conducted from a respectful distance following best practice advice and guidance.

When out and about around the coast be alert for marine life, particularly seals resting on rocks or beaches. Always aim to 'Watch Seals Well' and leave seals as you found them. Please make our coastline a haven for nature and remember:

- Give seals space
- Disturbance is harmful
- Put seals first
- Think seal

Please see page 99 for more information on watching seals well.

Sue was awarded an MBE in the King's New Year Honours list for services to Wildlife Protection and Conservation.

Cornwall Sustainability Award winners

SPOTTING THE SOUTHWEST'S SPECIAL SEALS

Grey seals live on both sides of the Atlantic Ocean – in the areas coloured yellow

Britain's largest land breeding marine mammal, grey seals (Halichoerus grypus) inhabit our wildest and most exposed rocky shores. They love the sensation of stormy white water, the primitive echoes of cliff backed coves with dark sea caves and the seclusion of remote sandy beaches. Their proper title is the north Atlantic grey seal, which describes their range extending from the eastern seaboard of the USA and

Canada, across the north Atlantic to western Europe from Scandinavia in the north, down to a southern limit of northwest France.

Just over a third of the entire world's grey seals live in UK waters and 90% of these are in Scotland. Despite this there are still fewer grey seals in the UK than red squirrels. Cornwall is at the hub of a genetically distinct sub population of Celtic seals from the Isle of Man, SW Ireland and Wales to the north to France in the south. Two common seals from Cornwall have also been identified as having come from Belgium and Holland. This makes the grey seals in Cornwall very special indeed.

Tolerance of such varied environmental conditions demonstrates a grey seal's adaptability. This gives hope for their continued survival during global warming with its multiple impacts. Rising sea levels and coastal retreat, however, will significantly affect their haul out and pupping sites, making their survival more challenging. The effective protection and maintenance of an interconnected network of grey seal habitat in Cornwall is critical for future generations of these unique creatures across the Celtic fringe.

Seal in harbour

WHERE TO SEE GREY SEALS IN CORNWALL

You can expect to see grey seals all around the Cornish Coast and in the Isles of Scilly. Of marine mammals, grey seals are unique in that they spend extended periods of time on land and may dry out fully with no ill effects. Whilst it is normal for them to spend a fifth of their lives on land, this makes grey seals extremely vulnerable to disturbance.

Boat trip to see seals

CSGRT research shows that seals are already suffering from chronic levels of disturbance – most of which is unintentional. For this reason the geographical locations of haul out and pupping sites have been omitted from this book. This is to protect seals from ever increasing levels of human presence and activity.

To get close to seals, you can visit the Cornish Seal Sanctuary at Gweek, where you will get better views of them than in the wild. Many boat trips to see seals are advertised widely in the local media and depart from Looe, Penzance, St Mary's, St Ives, Padstow and Newquay. Remember that most seals are likely to be seen hauled out on land around low tide. At high tide, good views of wild grey seals can be experienced in harbours, particularly in St Ives and Newquay. Please see pages 98-99 to understand why it is vital that seals are never fed in the wild, as this has many lifelong detrimental effects on their wellbeing. We strongly advise that you only use a 'Wildlife Safe' (WiSe) operator, checking their reviews online before booking and avoid deliberate encounters with seals in the sea.

SEAL SPECIES IN CORNWALL

Whilst most seals around our coast are grey seals, we do get other seal species. Common or harbour seals (Phoca vitulina) have been identified with increasing frequency. It pays to know the differences between these and the more numerous grey seals. Please email all your seal sightings to sightings@cornwallsealgroup.co.uk .

Grey seals are the larger and stronger of the two species, whilst common seals benefit from greater athletic agility. Overall, common seals tend to have a ringed or tiny dotted fur pattern, creating perfect camouflage for sheltered, seaweed covered rocky shores, whilst grey seals may be plain or blotched and spotty.

The easiest way to distinguish between the two seal species is to look carefully at their heads. In proportion to their bodies, common seals have relatively small heads with clear foreheads down to their shorter snouts with snub noses. From the front their heads are rounded and their nostrils form a distinct 'v' shape. In contrast, grey seals have much larger heads, with strong, flat profiled noses, which become more Romanesque as they get older. From the front, grey seals' heads form a vertical oval shape and their nostrils (except in juveniles) are much more parallel. Common seals' heads appear more cat like, whilst grey seals' heads look more like Labradors.

Common or harbour seal (left) with a grey seal (right)

At least two common seals are routinely sighted commuting along the south coast. Adult male 'Ellis' and female 'Serena Lowen' have been regularly identified since 2009 and 2015 respectively. In some years multiple common seal pups have been recorded and/or rescued right around the southwest coast by British Divers Marine Life Rescue for rehabilitation at the Cornish Seal Sanctuary. The origin of these pups is still unknown.

Other seal species seen in Cornish waters come from the Arctic – the hooded seal (Cystophora cristata) and harp seal (Pagophilus groenlandicus). It is interesting that when one species has appeared in Cornwall, so has the other. Both are spectacular species but very different in appearance.

Hooded seals, which are slightly bigger than grey seals, are named after the balloon like appendages that males can inflate on top of their noses. Adult harp seals are smaller seals and have a distinctive dark band that begins in a point at the front and top of their backs and that extends diagonally down both sides towards their rear flippers. Harp seal pups are the main focus for Canadian Seal Hunters. More recently a ringed seal

was rescued from a south coast harbour. Given away by its extra muscular appearance and feistier nature, this ringed seal was thought to have come from Svalbard in Scandinavia. Amazing!

Please always send seal records with a date and location to sightings@cornwallsealgroup. co.uk and photos are a bonus enabling us to give information back about your observation.

A harp seal (below) and a hooded seal (bottom)

ADAPTATIONS TO LIFE ON LAND AND IN THE SEA

Grey seals share their ancestry with cats, dogs, otters and bears and have characteristics in common with each of them. They are long-lived mammals with males thought to live to 25 years old in the wild and females living to over 30 years, with the oldest recorded wild female grey seal living to be 46 years old. In captivity, one of the oldest recorded grey seals achieved the grand old age of 40 – this was 'Magnus', who spent the last 18 years of his life at the Cornish Seal Sanctuary at Gweek. I have not been studying seals for long enough to know if the books are correct.

Grey seals are streamlined for life at sea, using alternating sideways movements of their powerful, webbed and fanned rear flippers to propel them through the water. Average swim speeds are around 4km an hour, but they are capable of incredible acceleration reaching top speeds of 25km an hour. A grey seal can swim 100km in a day and one young male seal satellite tagged in France swam

A seal's webbed rear flippers and tail

Clockwise from top left: A seal moving at speed

Powerful shoulders simultaneously throw both fore flippers forwards in front of the seal's body. Strong claws (supported by underling claw bones) grip the sand, rocks or weed. The muscle movements ripple through the seal's whole body propelling it forwards, not unlike a 'jack in the box' caterpillar.

Often described as ungainly on land, grey seals can move surprisingly quickly and can outrun all but the fastest adult human! It is at the junction of land and sea where a seal's marine instinct and terrestrial dexterous strength become apparent. Once the seal has decided to haul out, it will patrol offshore seeking a suitable haul out ramp or stretch of beach. Once selected, it will hang around just offshore apparently sensing and testing the movement of the water and waves before making its move.

the whole of the Cornish coast in 4 days. At speed their fore flippers are folded tight against their sides and a small muscular tail acts as a rudder. This helps them perform their equivalent of handbrake turns underwater.

Once out of the water and moving or hauling across land, a seal's fore flippers become the principal driving force of locomotion.

A seal will use its natural buoyancy and surf landwards on a wave as it swashes up the shore, even when this is a steep rock ledge. If needed, it then grips the slippery seaweed and limpet covered rocks with its 10 long and strong fore claws. Friction from maximum body contact with shore will help the seal to cling on as the backwash sucks down towards the sea. The seal clings on hoping not to be dragged back seaward. When the next wave hits, the seal is ready and reacts to its increased buoyancy by thrusting its whole body onwards and upwards in a cycle to be repeated until the seal is completely clear of the water. In this way a seal navigates a situation where humans would be ripped to shreds!

Hauling out is not to be rushed and neither is a seal's return to the sea. Seals prefer to haul out at higher tides and remain there until they are floated off by the next high tide. The sudden appearance of a person or a close approach will scare the seal. This results in a release of stress hormones along with raised heart and breathing rates. If the person backs off at this point, the seal will return to resting. A continued approach will, however, result in a flight response. Seals rushing off a beach is called a 'stampede' as seals hurriedly scramble seawards. They inevitably leave subtle trails of blood as they injure themselves on sharp rocks or as they rip out claws that get caught between rocks.

Seals unfortunate enough to be hauled high above the receding water line may take steep tumbles called 'tombstoning'. Sadly this can result in multiple broken bones with bottom jaws and ribs being the most likely breakages. Worse still, in summertime, heavily pregnant females carry their pups in their bellies. Stampeding or tombstoning can be particularly serious for them and their unborn pups. Whilst not obvious or visible to us humans, disturbance for a seal is always a waste of energy, sometimes results in injury and can occasionally be fatal.

As seals forage underwater, all their available oxygen is prioritised for their diving activity. Oxygen is necessary for healthy digestion, so a seal must wait until it returns to an oxygen rich environment at the surface or at a haul out to begin digesting its food. Seals can rest or sleep in the sea or on land. Seals are thought to shut down more of their brain when resting on land where they have to assess fewer variables. Seals may float vertically (bottling) or horizontally (logging)

Pregnant female high above the sea is very vulnerable to human disturbance

at the sea surface. Alternatively, they may haul out every few days to rest, aid the digestion of their food and replenish normal and emergency oxygen supplies. In addition, seals leave the sea more frequently and for longer periods during their annual moulting season (Winter/Spring) and pupping season (Autumn/Winter).

At the sea surface, a seal preparing to dive will use its muscles to open its nostrils to inhale and to exhale a few times before relaxing to close its nostrils (in total contrast to humans). Recent research shows that 15 seconds before diving, a seal will make an apparently conscious decision to dive and this is reflected in its physiology. Blood is withdrawn from its periphery and pooled into its core (heart, lungs and brain) and its heart rate slows from around 120 to as few as 4 beats a minute. This effectively shuts off their circulation. Immediately before diving a seal will forcefully expel the air from its lungs and duck its head lower than its tail and use its hind quarters to propel itself downwards. Breathing out before diving, and taking no air on dives, prevents a seal suffering from decompression sickness, or the bends, as a result of pressure changes when returning to the surface.

On average, grey seals are reported to dive to around 60m and for up 9 minutes, but have been recorded diving to depths of 200m and for longer if needed. During this time, oxygen is stored in the haemoglobin and myoglobin in blood and muscles. Seals are tolerant to the build up of lactic acid. The deeper and longer the dive, the longer the seal must rest at the surface or on land to repay its oxygen debt.

Seals' adaptations to the cold are a little more obvious. A blubber layer between 6 to 10cm thick in adults provides insulation and 2 layers of dense fur help to reduce wind chill on land. Most heat is lost through a seal's extremities, its face and flippers, which have little blubber. A dry, hauled out seal being splashed by a rising tide feels the cold water most at its extremities, which results in 'bananaing'. This is a characteristic behavioural reaction, where

Female seal bananaing (above) and seal bottling and yawning (top)

Seal bananaing with rear flippers extended

the seal lifts its head and tail up in an arc at the same time! This keeps a seal's sensitive bits out of the cold water for as long as possible. (See behaviour section).

This can be taken to extremes and I have even seen a seal get floated off a rock in a banana shape. Eventually gravity results in the inevitable, with rear flippers dropping below the surface first and finally the head dropping beneath the surface. Seals 'bottling' at the surface may even have dry faces from a prolonged sleep. Given a choice, seals acclimatise themselves before fully re-entering the sea. On a hot day this might even involve dipping their head briefly underwater and raising it back up repeatedly before committing itself to leaving the land. A seal's flippers possess counter current heat exchange systems where veins wrap around arteries recapturing warmth and returning it with blood back to the body. In contrast, seals hauled out in direct summer sunshine may overheat because of their effective insulation. At such times, seals may splay their webbing wide on both rear flippers, exposing them to the air and cold sand to maximise heat loss. Digging like a turtle on a beach to reach cooler sand may additionally aid heat loss.

SEAL SENSES

Touch

When feeding, particularly in waters with poor visibility, a seal's most important sense is probably feeling vibrational movement in the sea picked up by their whiskers or vibrissae. A seal may be sensitive to the movement of fish several minutes ahead of it. As a seal dries out on land, its vibrissae curl gracefully at the ends. A seal has between 3 and 6 (though usually 4/5) pairs of eyebrows, over 40 pairs of whiskers and 2 single hairs (rhinal vibrissae) on top and either side of its nose – presumably for fine tuning directional vibrations. Each whisker has 1500 nerve endings in comparison to the 2500 in our hands – making their muzzles super sensitive.

Each whisker has a spiral cross section that is thought to transfer water from root to tip. The spirals also reduce vortices developing behind them which would pull the whiskers backwards. New science has shown that much like a kestrel's head being stationary when hunting whilst the rest of its body is in motion, muscle movements hold a seal's whiskers in position even when water resistance should push them backwards. Only with whiskers can seals detect fish movement vibrations in the water column. Increased silt in the water column washed down by rivers after storms makes it harder for seals to forage, which can be particularly serious for seals under 18 months of age.

Sight

Grey seals are thought to navigate using a combination of their senses. One of the most evocative features of a seal is its eyes; deep black pools that gaze at your soul! Large apertures capture more light in murky depths but increase the possibilities of damage. Protection comes from regular secretions that cover their corneas. A healthy, well hydrated seal will 'cry' constant tears forming damp 'panda' patches around their eyes.

Whilst a seal's eye is designed to see underwater, seals appear to be able to see movements even across great distances, for example between themselves and a cliff top, so keeping out of sight and maintaining a low profile on the skyline are particularly important ways of reducing disturbance. Designed to focus underwater, seals have two adaptations of a vertical slit pupil and a horizontally flattened cornea that enable them to have amphibious vision and see almost as well in air as through water. Even blind seals have been known to survive in the wild, so their other senses must compensate for their loss of sight.

Sound

The 18 true seal species are defined by having no ear flaps. This is an adaptation to living in colder waters where ear flaps would result in too much heat loss. Despite this, grey seals have very sensitive hearing with a similar range of pitches to humans. Juveniles seem to be particularly good at hearing high pitched sounds. Seals can even hear people on a distant clifftop and will spook at loud voices or unusual sounds such as dog barks. Although complicated by ambient sound levels, wind direction, wind strength and echoes from rocky cliffs, seals have been known to hear an approaching engine before a human.

With boats they are particularly attuned to changing engine or paddle sounds. Natural 'predator response' instincts warn the seal that anything stopping near them could be a dangerous predator taking an interest in them. So, it is best to keep moving slowly past any seal you have spotted as this will avoid being a 'red flag' provoking the seal's natural instinct to flee. This will result in lengthening the magical moment you have of observing an awesome marine mammal behaving naturally in the wild. We should always aim to leave seals as and where we find them.

Smell

Careful observation of a wild seal reveals just how important the sense of smell is to them. A seal mum will instantly recognise the smell of her own pup, recoiling immediately from the scent of another pup approached in error. A seal surfacing nearby will invariably open its nostrils to deliberately catch a whiff of your scent to work out what you are.

Young seals can be seen sand snuffling (see behaviours section). It seems seals smell you first, hear you second and then finally see you. So, seals may be alert to your presence before you are even aware they are there. A newly hauled out seal will greet others by sniffing the snouts and ears of other seals. This presumably helps them identify who is

who in the world. It is even possible that seals can sense hormonal or pheromonal changes in other seals and people. Like other animals, for example horses and dogs, seals appear able to tell when people are nervous of them and respond more mischievously as a result.

Communication
Verbal
Seals communicate with each other vocally and can often be heard howling around our coasts. Often described as 'singing' these high-pitched howls sound like lengthy 'woohooing'. The truth is less romantic. These vocalisations occur when one seal hauls out close to another. A personal space violation will prompt a 'woohoo' response, usually accompanied by much fore flippering. The majority of these vocalisations are produced by females, who can have surprisingly loud voices that carry evocatively on the wind.

Males on the other hand vocalise but with much deeper voices that more resemble growls and hisses. These are usually reserved for each other during pecking order altercations or when well matched males confront each other in a power struggle. Underwater communications have been recorded that resemble deep guttural grunts that appear to send blasts of sound into the water column. Divers in their proximity describe these as being powerful enough to vibrate right through their chest cavity.

A more recently described adult male behaviour is communing, where groups of males appear to gather underwater nose to nose vocalising, but the purpose of this behaviour is not yet known. A more obvious communication occurs between mums and their pups. A mum will respond to the call of her pup who vocalises when hungry; what is so amazing is this pup call actually does sound like an elongated 'muuum'.

Non verbal: Body language
Observation of encounters between seals suggests that they are also able to read each other's body language. A look from one seal can elicit a response from another many metres away. Clearly there is much for us to learn about the complexities of seal society. (Read more in the story of 'W' on page 86).

KNOWING WHAT YOU'RE LOOKING AT

A grey seal's coat of many colours. A grey seal's selection box.

Contrary to the image conjured up by their name, grey seals exhibit huge natural variation. Their colours range from black to white and cream to chocolate with all colour combinations in between.

Seal pups under the age of three weeks have soft, long white fur coats that are lost through a process of moulting around the time of weaning. Pale, plain coloured seals are often wrongly described as pups, even when they are very large.

Grey seals are described as pups up to three weeks old, thereafter they are moulted pups or weaners. Juveniles up to the age of four years have a thinner more streamlined appearance. Between four and five years old, seals suddenly balloon outwards, becoming much fatter as sub adults. Up to adulthood, seals can be aged approximately by their length. After the age of seven, their age can only be estimated from observations of their nose profiles which become more convex or 'roman' with increasing age.

Smallish honey or ginger coloured plain seals are juveniles, going through an elongated first

A classically marked adult male seal (left), and a 'girly' young male (right)

A classically marked adult female seal (left), and a plain dark adult female (right)

annual moult. Seal fur is very soft and replaced every year during the annual late winter and spring moult, after which seals look their most pristinely beautiful as they sport their brand new fur coats. A pup's first annual moult takes place at three weeks, so this is its first annual moult done. Their second does not take place for over 12 months and more likely 18 months later. So, their fur apparently breaks down and loses its pigment turning them plain golden brown and making them almost impossible to identify.

As a species, grey seals are sexually dimorphic. This means that males look very different from females. Males average 2.3m, with larger males up to 3 metres long (although the longest grey seal recorded by the Cornwall Wildlife Trust Marine Strandings Network was 2.8 metres) and weighing in at between 230 and 300 kilograms. Females are smaller growing up to 2 metres long and 180 kilograms. Dimensions do not tell the whole story, as older seals are not always longer or fatter.

The easiest way to work out the gender of a seal from distance is to look at its belly! On the underside of their lower abdomen, all seals have an umbilicus 'belly button' mark and 2 nipples between this and their rear flippers. Male seals have an additional aperture called a prepuce (sometimes highlighted by a linear worn patch from

Heads of adult grey seals: male (left) and female (right)

the prepuce down towards the seal's rear flippers). If the seal is uncooperative and lying on its belly, then you are generally advised to look at the seal's overall appearance of its fur or pelage pattern. On two imaginary pelage pattern spectrums from dark to light and plain to spotty, adult male seals tend to be darker and plainer, whilst females tend to be lighter and spottier. This holds true for about 80% of seals, but there are exceptions to confound us all! Only females have really light spotty bellies!

Another way of distinguishing male from female seals is to look at their heads. Male grey seals have far longer and broader snouts than females of the same age. Females have much smaller heads with finer facial features – they are effectively prettier! In addition, older males tend to get a more

exaggerated convex nose profile than older females. Dominant breeding males (called 'beachmasters') develop a ruff of extra fat deposits and wrinkles around their necks which are thicker. This 'mane' protects them whilst they are sparring with other males for access rights to females. 'Beachmasters' often look battle worn from the scars inflicted by other wannabe 'beachmaster' males.

As grey seals get older, they grow lengthways. They all begin life covered in long white fluffy fur called a lanugo, which was thought to have given them camouflage when they were born on winter snow and ice. If this was true, given the length of time since the last ice age in the UK, it is hard to understand why seals have not evolved to lose this white coat, especially given the speed that seals appear to be adapting over our 20 years of study. Perhaps the white coat serves another purpose – our best guess being that of protection from wind chill? Seals under 3 weeks of age will keep varying amounts of their white coats. These begin to be lost (moulting) at different rates for different pups – some are fully moulted into their adult pelage pattern at two weeks, whilst others by 4 weeks will still have tufts of white fur left.

White-coated pup (top) and golden-brown juvenile (bottom)

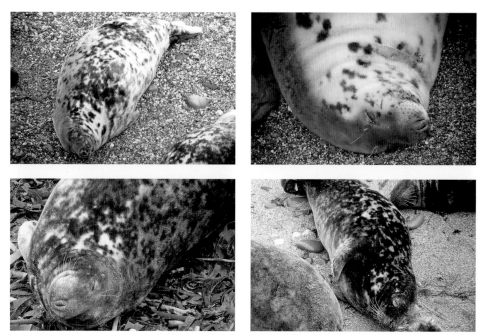

Four distinctive fur patterns, clockwise from top left: 'Black Rabbit', 'Parallels', 'Pacific' and 'Lost Boy'

Each seal has a unique fur pattern, as distinctive as a fingerprint, from which it can be individually identified. Work that I began has prompted CSGRT teams across the region to do the same. Volunteers spend many hours inventing pictures from their fur patterns, similar to visualising images in clouds and ink blots. Names are inspired by creative imaginations applied to a seal's fur pattern. This is made more challenging by the fact that different people 'see' different things reflected there!

A seal's fur pattern remains the same for life, although the contrast within the pattern may change over time as the seal ages. As males

Seals moulting

age, their pattern contrast decreases making it harder to identify them. Female fur patterns increase in contrast making them more distinctive and easier to identify over time. The clarity of all seals' fur patterns diminishes during their annual moult. Pigments in the old fur break down turning the fur brown and it is pushed out of hair follicles by fresh 'high definition' black, grey and white new fur growing beneath. Likewise, seal patterns can be masked by a seal's love of rolling around on sandy beaches which disguises its identity! Sleek wet fur lies flush and smoothly against a seal's body making fur patterns crystal clear as they emerge from the sea to haul onto land. Exposed to air, the fur begins to stand on end, perpendicular to the seal's skin as it dries, blurring patterns that seep into each other.

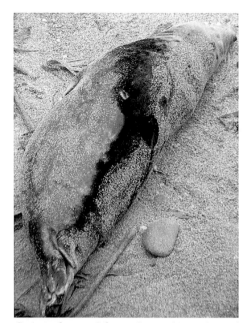

Clockwise from top left: a seal covered in sand; a seal with dry fur; the same seal with wet fur; a wet and dry seal

Photo identification of seals enables CSGRT citizen scientists to unobtrusively follow individual seals throughout their lives across time and space and it is this work that reveals many secrets about the private lives of seals around our coast and beyond.

GREY SEALS' SECRET LIVES

Watching individual seals grow up is a real privilege, witnessing the key events for them is very special and watching a new life begin is an awe-inspiring experience. A seal's calendar is divided up differently to ours and seals seem to live through three main seasons a year. All are key to their survival as a species:

• *The pupping season:* this begins in August and continues until December, although white coated seal pups have been observed in every month of the calendar year in Cornwall. Since our first surveys, the pupping season has moved earlier and become shorter, so most pups are now born in September and October (when I began it was October and November).

• *The moulting season:* this overlaps with the pupping season and begins as adults finish breeding and continues until May. Females moult first followed by males, and juveniles can even be seen moulting in the summer. Seals are at their most grumpy and craggy as they lose and replace all their fur which saps huge amounts of their energy.

• *The offshore foraging season:* seals feed all year round, but their main period for focusing on food and fattening up is between June and August in readiness for breeding. At this time, the mainland haul out beaches are used less, in favour of more remote offshore haul outs, which become popular as they are presumably closer to rich foraging grounds.

The Pupping Season

'Kelp's' birth

One unspectacular late September Monday morning, Simon and I were lying on a cliff edge peering at the reasonable sized haul out of seals beneath us. There was plenty of activity to keep us entertained with around 40 seals. 'Beachmaster' 'W' was calmly in control, keeping the testosterone levels of all wannabe 'beachmasters' such as 'S Hook' and 'Feathers' at bay. We had felt honoured to watch Mum 'Walking Fingers' feed her pup 'Treasure' and all was well with the world.

As I routinely scanned my binoculars across the beach, I noticed something unusual out of

'Kelp', clockwise from top left: being born; shortly after birth; an hour old; being fed at three days old

the corner of one eye. One of the seals was quivering in a strange fashion. Seals often shiver as they emerge from the sea, but this wasn't really a shiver, just more of a quiver! We had already talked about the seal in question, as she was an unusually dark female, being milk chocolate colour all over with just a few white markings and she was heavily pregnant, very very heavily pregnant! Seals are generally fattest around their waists, but pregnant females are usually obvious, being fattest around their lower abdomen and carrying a lot of excess blubber all over from their necks downwards.

We had a brief conversation about moving around the cliff top to get a closer look, but feared we might miss something in the short time this would take and were suddenly distracted by another cliff top onlooker, whose barking dog scared a lot of the seals into the sea. Cursing, we looked back at the quivering seal, who despite being nearest to the disturbance was one of the only seals not to have shifted an inch.

At that moment her contractions began, about 3 sets of 4 big contractions. As we watched, a small white 'tennis ball' emerged between her rear flippers and expanded to the size of a football, before being suddenly sucked back in. The mother seal looked surprised and turned her head to look for a pup, but none was there, so she settled for the next contractions. One more set and the football returned, the pup emerged head first (though seals are so streamlined with no long appendages pups can be born either way round). As its rear flippers flopped out last and spun round, the umbilicus twanged and snapped easily.

A new born pup, still in its intact sac, was lying prone and still on the beach. A few nerve-racking milliseconds passed before the pup suddenly twitched, stretching its neck forwards, opening its mouth and splitting the sac over the top of its unsteady head. What a shock it must be to leave a wonderfully warm, dark space for a cold hard beach on a bright September day! A series of sneezes helped the pup 'Kelp' to clear its passages and take its first breath of life! We were speechless! We had not witnessed a seal pup birth before, nor have we seen one since.

The next few hours would be critical to 'Kelp's' wellbeing. Pups seem to be born on outgoing tides, giving them a precious 12 hours to acclimatise to their surroundings. Nourished immediately prior to birth, 'Kelp' was not hungry and didn't want feeding. First feeds are notoriously anxious times and 'Kelp's' instinct drew him to his mother a few hours later. His lack of previous experience of suckling left him at a loss about what to do. 'Kelp's' Mum carefully manoeuvred to place her body in exactly the right spot for 'Kelp' to suckle, but he was more interested in following the stronger scent of her flippers and head, leading him to move in entirely the wrong direction.

All this made for 30 minutes of very painful viewing for us...will he? ...won't he? Everything depended on 'Kelp's' ability to find the life saving, nutrient rich, over 50% fat, first milk from his mother that would protect him with natural immunity! After many near misses, 'Kelp' finally latched on to first one and then the other of his

Mum's teats. It was almost as if he expanded in size as his rolls of skin filled with the volume of milk he consumed. Audible gasps were heard from the cliff top as we finally remembered to breathe again!

The bond between pup and mother is strong (top), the mother's milk is 50 percent fat (above)

Most newborn pups weigh in at around 13-14 kilograms and are about a metre long mass of baggy skin and bone. Rolls of skin give a misleading impression of health, but they are ready for the exponential growth that a pup will make in its first 3 weeks of life. Pups that are a few days old have an obvious umbilicus of varying length that will change from bright pink to black before drying, shrivelling up and falling off. Pups look their most photogenic up to 3 days old, but they are very vulnerable. Should high tides and big swells drag them seawards, they would struggle to survive. In contrast, pups over 3 days old can cope with swimming in all but the worst sea conditions under their mother's attentive supervision.

The bond between mother and pup is very strong and a mother can instantly tell her pup with a call or a sniff! Pups feed a little and more often to begin with, averaging once every four hours for a few minutes as a result of their tiny stomachs. They will then feed less frequently every 7 or so hours and for longer periods as they near weaning at 15 to 21 days. By the end of the second week pups look like fat torpedoes and, after 3 weeks they resemble barrels, so fat they must dig a hole in the sand to rest their heads! At around 40kg, they are weaned and

without any demonstrations from Mum, hunger guides them to the sea, where they must head out into the harsh world of the open ocean and teach themselves to feed. We must assume that pups learn to do this from a mixture of 'trial and error' and 'show and tell' from watching other seals they encounter.

Mum on the other hand is left exhausted from rearing her pup. Having remained close to her pup, on the beach, in the sea cave or keeping a line of sight to her pup from the sea for three weeks, she has been prevented from proactively feeding herself. As her pup has put on 30+ kilograms, Mum's fasting means she has lost a third of her body weight. Her protruding hip bones show just how emaciated she is. Despite not looking her best, Mum is her most attractive at this time to the dominant 'beachmaster' seal who mates with her on land or in the sea.

Having noisily and assertively resisted the 'beachmaster's' advances for up to 3 weeks, the female will finally accept his approach at around the time her pup is weaned. Manoeuvring his belly to her back, the business of mating appears to take place quickly. The two seals will then lie quietly together. Several mating pairs have been observed intertwined and motionless restfully on land or at the surface of the sea for over 20 minutes. As the floating pair occasionally roll over, the female will scull with her fore flippers to enable them both to breathe restfully at the surface.

The land-based pair robustly put up with being buffeted repeatedly by the incoming waves and being wrapped up in a seaweed duvet. Seals appear their most serene at this time. Our photo ID work has also revealed that some females will mate several times with

'Missee', a day-old pup, with her exhausted mother

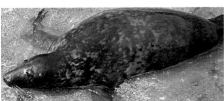

Clockwise from top left: 'Rocket' Day 1; Day 5; Day 16; Day 21; Day 31; at 17 months

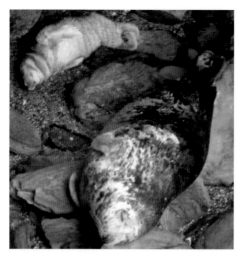

In three weeks, 'Storm' grows as his mother shrinks

one male in the same day or over two consecutive days. Mums have also been seen heading out to sea with a 'sneaky' male whilst the 'beachmaster' is otherwise engaged (sleeping or mating with another female). Other mums are picky about who they mate with – see 'Ghost's' story below.

Unable to sustain a pregnancy in her worn out state, the female's fertilised egg divides a few times, before becoming dormant in a process called delayed implantation. If, over the next 3 months, Mum feeds well and regains her health, strength and weight, the blastocyst implants in the womb lining and continues to develop normally and her pregnancy begins again! In effect, seal Mums can be pregnant 24/7 for their entire breeding lives. Common sense suggests they may take occasional years off, presumably when food is in shorter supply. With a gestation period of around 8 months from the point of implantation, seal Mums tend to give birth to their pups at roughly the same time every year.

'Ghost' a world record breaking mum

One adult female seal 'Ghost' is our most special mum! She appeared with her first pup on 3rd November, which she successfully weaned. 'Ghost' then delighted us by returning every year to the same beach to give birth to new pups, getting earlier and earlier. Finally, her birthing date became predictable between 7th to 15th October. Sadly, her sixth pup called 'Shadow' was one of three pups to die on the same night in very high Spring tides in stormy seas. This is a common occurrence repeated during every pupping season storm, washing pups away from their mothers right around the coast.

Storm Brian in 2017 was thought to have separated pretty much every pup from its mother in a single night during a high Spring tide. Messing up hormonal triggers and causing health complications, Storm Brian had far reaching consequences the following pupping season. 2018 had a 46% drop in pup numbers across Cornwall. 'Ghost' was one of those mums we didn't see that year – the only year she has not returned to Cornwall.

'Shadow's' dead body remained at the back of the beach above the high tide line. Despite being scavenged, 'Ghost's' instinct to look after a pup she could smell was so strong, that she returned to try and feed her dead pup for the next 15 days. Sadly 'Ghost's' 10th pup 'Polo' did not survive either. It too died on the first high tide after being born. Its sad floating body taught us how heavy a seal pup skull is. As the

heaviest part of a pup's body the skull sinks below the surface but stays afloat because of a buoyant belly full of gas.

As waves swash the little body back and forth in the shallows, the head catches on the seabed breaking the neck. This, along with scavenging through soft tissue openings in the head, means many dead pups are found headless on beaches as part of the natural cycle of decomposition. Grey seal pup mortality rates are reportedly high with 15% dying in the first three weeks with an additional 40 to 60% dying in the next 18 months. Such is the savageness of living where open ocean meets land.

'Ghost's' no show in 2018 made us worried that she might have died. You can imagine how delighted we were when she returned the following year fat, fit and healthy. In total, 'Ghost' has given birth to an amazing 19 pups in 20 years! What a wonderful mum! Long may this continue.

After seal pups leave the beach of their birth, their natal site, they are thought to explore their new underwater world, during a period in their life referred to as a post weaning dispersal. Inept feeders to begin with, young pups will eat anything and lose a lot of weight

'Ghost's' 2022 pup called 'Poodle'

before gaining some as they become more competent hunters. A year-old seal is only distinguishable from a recently weaned pup in its length, as it is unlikely to be much fatter. This is why mortality rates are so high up to the age of 18 months.

Unlike 'Ghost', not all seal mums have read their 'pupping manual' which says they should give birth where they themselves were born. Some mums pup at a similar location each year depending on site availability. Other mums will have pups at several sites, hundreds of kilometres apart and even in multiple Celtic Sea countries! For example, 'Waves' has had 7 pups at 3 different sites. We have known 'Tulip Belle' since 2001 and thanks to the Manx Wildlife Trust, we discovered she has commuted between Cornwall and the Isle of Man where she has had at least four seal pups....that is a round trip of 900 kilometres each time!

'Wings' is one of a handful of mums who have pupped in two different countries. 'Wings' was recorded by the Wildlife Trust of South and West Wales with a pup on the island of Skomer and she has since pupped multiple times in Cornwall. You can see from her visit calendar (page 52) that 'Wings' starts

and ends the year at the West Cornwall site, spends the summer in St Ives Bay, swims up to Skomer in Pembrokeshire and perhaps spends the late spring on the south coast of Cornwall.

Female seals: 'Ghost' (bottom) and her 2022 pup called 'Poodle' (top)

'Rocket' now 15 years old (left) and mature adult 'Wings' (right)

On leaving the beach, seal pups are thought to make mental maps of the marine world they visit and some pups swim hundreds of kilometres in their first year. One seal pup satellite tagged by the Sea Mammal Research Unit in north Wales swam to Rosslare in SE Ireland, the Isles of Scilly and visited a few kilometres off the Brittany coast before returning to the south coast of Cornwall. She completed a journey of around 1000 kilometres by the ripe old age of 3 months old! In Cornwall, so far, just 2 pups have been observed to return to their natal site and both 17 months after they left.

These 2 special seals are 'Curly' and 'Rocket'. 'Curly's' return is particularly significant, as being female, it will be interesting to see if she chooses to have her pups in the area she was born, but we must wait at least 7 years to find this out! 'Rocket' on the other hand has been seen every year since at multiple north coast sites and has even been observed Beachmastering from the age of 10 onwards.

From 18 months on, the juvenile years of a seal appear relaxed and anxiety free. Naturally playful, young seals are frequently observed interacting with each other and generally disturbing the older adult seals who prefer to sleep on the haul out beach.

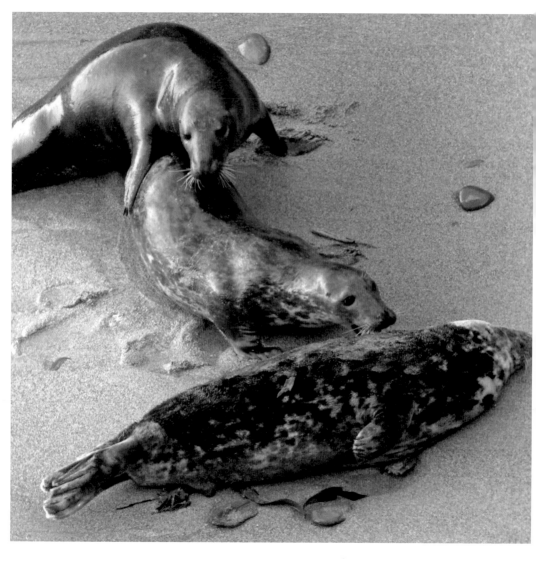

Two wet juveniles playing on the beach, about to wake up a dry 'White ring teddy stripe'! He got the shock of his life! (opposite), Juveniles playing in shallow water (above)

Seals' 'sniff greetings' appear to inform them about friends and foes. Friends may be seen in pairs or small groups rolling around at the water's edge, especially during the breeding season, practising the moves that they will need as adults. Foes may trigger flight responses, as seals rush away, splashing into the shallows and doing a beach start from 0 to 60 in no time, as rear flippers thrash from side to side propelling the seal into the safety of deeper water. Much of this play is mischievous and involves a lot of body contact.

Most adult male seals are non breeding and barely register it is the breeding season. Each seal pupping location has a dominant male, referred to as the 'beachmaster'. Strong leadership from the 'beachmaster' results in a calm haul out, where all the seals respect who is boss. Insecure leaders with poor leadership skills may result in anxiety ridden haul outs, frequently disturbed by marauding wannabe males challenging the 'beachmaster' in fearsome fights, albeit short in duration. Sleeping seals are forced to scatter as sparring males move obliviously around the haul out disturbing everyone.

Females always protest. Adult females appear to be the only seals capable of dominating the 'beachmasters'. As a female's personal space is invaded, she will invariably howl a loud warning at the interloper signalling him to leave. If he doesn't leave her alone, she will continue howling, using her fore flippers to repeatedly swat him and lunging her neck forward to snap at him! Most 'beachmasters' understand this message loud and clear and communicate their lack of threat and subservience by slowing rolling away before backing off to leave the female to sleep soundly!

Mother 'Walking Fingers', father 'W' and pup 'Treasure'

Only a few adult males become a 'beachmaster', winning them the chance to pass on their genes to future generations, and the cleverest 'beachmasters' will dominate a haul out over several years, fathering all the pups from that location. As a result of a year separating mating and birth and the difficulties of spotting pups at breeding locations, only a few times have photos been taken showing a Mum, Dad and Pup on the beach together at one time.

Surprisingly, 'beachmasters' are not always the biggest or strongest males. Rather we presume they are the worldliest wise – perhaps they have the biggest brains? It is possible that seals work out a pecking order through the interactions they have as juveniles. The best 'beachmasters' know when to leave pupping females alone, saving precious energy reserves, and will only try their luck at mating as she comes into season. As this happens, he will assert his authority. He'll clear all other potential competitive males off the haul out and leave males he can easily dominate, females and juveniles to sleep in peace, so minimising disruption.

To remain dominant for all or part of a pupping season, a 'beachmaster' must meet several criteria. He will have to stay on his territory and therefore fast to avoid leaving it to feed. He must treat all his potential female partners with care and respect and show endless patience as he waits for them to tolerate his advances. During potential encounters with rival males, he must assess the best time to take control – for example as a big wave hits moving him into a position of strength higher up the beach than his challenger.

Some mature males and females will demonstrate a bond with each other over and above that imposed on them by territorial rights. 'White Back C' and 'Ghost' mated between 2011 and 2015. As an older male over the age of 22, 'White Back C' did not have the energy to 'beachmaster' for a season, he would simply return to protect 'Ghost' whilst she was with her pup. She would reject the advances of any other male and would only allow 'White Back C' to mate with her when the time was right and then they would both disappear. Such are the complexities of a seal society ruled by females!

THE MOULTING SEASON

Moulting seal

Late winter and early spring see the largest haul outs of seals on mainland sites, as seals spend less time at sea. Females moult after pupping and before males, but there is an overlap and huge numbers of scruffy looking seals litter our shores at this time of year. As the pigments are lost when their old fur breaks down, pelages take on a browner and plainer appearance.

Blood vessels near the skin's surface open their widest to fuel the growth of new grey fur beneath the old brown coat. Seals appear irritable and tetchy with each other during their moult. Frequent scratching with long sharp fore claws often results in broken and bleeding skin at this time of year. Re-scratched, the blood transfers to the flippers and into arc shaped lines on other areas of the seal's body as blood is spread during scratch after scratch. A seal with a superficial wound begins to look like a horror movie victim!

Moulting has a huge energetic cost. With blood so close to the surface of their skin, seals are particularly vulnerable at this time to human disturbance and cold shock from entering the sea too quickly without acclimatising. Although losing heat, energy can be conserved by hauling out and sleeping deeply on land. Being disturbed into the sea prematurely during the moulting season can be particularly expensive to a seal's energy budget, compromising the seals nutritional state for the rest of the year.

Cornwall Wildlife Trust's Marine Strandings Network reports show a secondary peak in seal deaths in April. This could be explained by seals who have not survived the energy loss through their annual moult. Whilst pupping season is the riskiest time for all breeding seals (all adult females and a small number of 'beachmasters'), moulting season is the most challenging time to survive for all seals after the age of 18 months.

THE OFFSHORE FORAGING SEASON

As summer approaches, seals begin to leave their mainland haul out sites, favouring the many more remote offshore rocky islands around the coast. These sites are only easily accessed in calmer sea conditions. Specific rock ledges vary according to the position of access ramps at the particular tidal state when a seal chooses to haul out. Often limited by the amount of resting space available, seal congregations tend to be smaller. Seals are thought to spend one in every four or five days hauled out to rest and digest the food caught in offshore foraging trips.

Moulting seal with blood transfer around the eye

Seals may travel from one haul out to the next, travelling long distances around the coast, or use a single haul out as a base for all their foraging trips. Some of these offshore haul outs have regular seals who may spend around 7 months at the site (for example 'Duchess' between February and August in Southeast Cornwall or Starfish from April to October in North Devon). For the mainland beach visitors, this is the hardest time of year to keep tabs on the seals and there is so much still to learn about where they go, although we do get regular insights.

'Woody' a summer holiday commuter

'Woody' is a juvenile male seal, who needed to be rescued from Sennen as a fully moulted weaner at a couple of months old. Rehabilitated by the marvellous Animal Care Team at the Cornish Seal Sanctuary, 'Woody' made good progress being released 4 months later from Portreath. Within a month 'Woody' had been spotted by Cornwall Seal Group Research Trust thriving back in the wild, where he has been observed regularly ever since. At the age of 3, 'Woody' was recorded as 'going on his holidays'! In late April he was identified at a north coast haul out in West Cornwall. By early June, 'Woody' was photographed by Bex Allen as he swam west of Newquay and by the end of June, 'Woody' was

captured on an underwater camera by Keith Hiscock off the south east coast of Lundy. By the end of August, 'Woody's' foraging trip was over and he was seen back where he started.

Little is known about the complexity of individual seal visits to particular sites, but seals appear to have seasonally repeated visit patterns. Some seals will visit a site only during the offshore foraging season, a number only during the moulting season and others for the breeding season. Some seals will stay for 2 of the 3 seal seasons and a few seals may remain all year round. What appears to be emerging from our extensive dataset on individual seal movements is that each is unique. Seals take solitary journeys between haul out sites where they meet up with other

'Woody' in north Cornwall (above), and off Lundy (right), showing ID tag circled in yellow

seals for the sociability and security of a group when they are most vulnerable on land.

Seal visit patterns are made all the more complex as the patterns change with the lifecycle stage of each seal. For example, one juvenile female seal 'Zigzag' visited a haul out site for four years only during the foraging season, but as she matured to breeding age, her visit pattern changed completely. She is now most reliably sighted during the moulting season and was pretty much absent during the foraging season. This pattern has persisted during adulthood and since 2015 she has been found at the West Penwith haul out site during the summer. Occasionally we have seen her with a pup. Despite being instantly recognisable, there were 2 years when she was a complete no show.

For three years, a juvenile male seal 'Flying bird' only visited the West Cornwall haul out briefly during the moulting and breeding seasons, before changing his visits as he

S112	2003	2004	2005	2006	2007	2008	2009	2010	2011	2012	2013	2014	2015	2016	2017	2018	2019	2020	2021	2022	Total
Jan																					0
Feb																					0
Mar																					0
Apr																					0
May																					0
Jun																					0
Jul																					0
Aug																					0
Sep								1													1
Oct		1	6	5	7	3	7	5	2	3	4	2	4	9	5		2	16	1	3	85
Nov	4	2		1																	7
Dec																					0
Total	4	3	6	6	7	3	7	6	2	3	4	2	4	9	5	0	2	16	1	3	93

S89	2003	2004	2005	2006	2007	2008	2009	2010	2011	2012	2013	2014	2015	2016	2017	2018	2019	2020	2021	2022	Total
Jan						2	2			3	1	1	2	1	1		1	1	1	1	18
Feb							2			1	1				1	1		1	3		10
Mar				1								2			2	1				1	7
Apr			1							1							1			1	4
May	1		1															1		1	4
Jun																1	1			2	4
Jul					1	2	1		1					1	1	3	10	3	1	3	29
Aug					2	1	1							1	4	9	11	12	12	4	57
Sep					1	1	1		2			1			3	9	1	2	3		24
Oct					3	1				1		2	1	2	2	12	4	6	1	4	41
Nov	1		1		1	1	2	6	3		2	4	1	2	2	4	3	1	1	1	43
Dec			1				2		1	5	1	3			1	2	2		1	1	21
Total	2	0	2	2	9	8	9	6	7	6	10	13	7	7	25	38	27	36	23	14	262

S5	2000	2001	2002	2003	2004	2005	2006	2007	2008	2009	2010	2011	2012	2013	2014	2015	2016	2017	2018	2019	2020	2021	2022	Total
Jan						1		2	1	1		1	1	2	1						1	1	1	14
Feb						1	1		2	5			2	1	1	1	1			1	2	1		19
Mar										2		1			1	1			1	1		1	1	9
Apr						1			1	1				2		2			2	1	1			11
May		2		1				1													2			6
Jun			1												1									2
Jul	1	1													1				1		1			5
Aug	1	1				2									1									5
Sep	1									2				4							1			8
Oct														1	2	1								4
Nov								1														1		2
Dec										1				1	2					2	1	1		8
Total	3	4	1	1	0	5	1	4	5	11	0	1	2	10	6	10	3	1	5	4	7	6	3	93

S7	2000	2001	2002	2003	2004	2005	2006	2007	2008	2009	2010	2011	2012	2013	2014	2015	2016	2017	2018	2019	2020	2021	2022	Total
Jan		2			1		2	2			1				1			1		1		1	1	13
Feb											1			1	2	1		1		1	1	1	1	10
Mar						2	4	1		1		1		1	1		1	1		3	1	1		18
Apr					5	9	2	7	1	1		1		5	1	3	1		2	2		1	3	44
May			1		2	3	1	4	1	2	1	1		3		4	2				1	1		27
Jun	1			1		3		1	1				1				2	3		1				14
Jul			1								1		1			1	1	1	1				1	9
Aug			1		5	5	1	1	2	1	2	1	2	3	3		1		1	2	6	1	3	41
Sep	1				4	5	8	3	2	2	3	3	3	2	5	2	6	2	1		2			54
Oct				3	9	14	4	2	1	3	4			3	5	1	6		2	2	3	3	1	67
Nov				4	4	5	5	1		2		1	1	4	2		1			1		2		33
Dec	1			3	1	6	1			1			1											14
Total	3	2	3	11	31	53	28	23	7	15	11	11	8	22	18	12	19	8	10	12	16	11	10	344

S262	2007	2008	2009	2010	2011	2012	2013	2014	2015	2016	2017	2018	2019	2020	2021	2022	Total
Jan																	0
Feb											2	1		1			4
Mar							1				2	1	3	2	3		12
Apr								1	4	2	4	2	2	1	2	1	19
May								1	2	1				5	2	2	13
Jun						1	2			6	6	7	5	11	8	2	56
Jul						2	6	3	4	6	8	12	2	14	6	7	70
Aug				3		9	6	4	7	7	13	6	7	7	4	4	74
Sep	1	1 6	1	2	2	1 2	5	3 2	6	3 5	1 2	1	3	5	6	1	60
Oct	9		4	1	1 2				3	1			2	1			24
Nov																	0
Dec				2			1	1	2			1	1	1			8
Total	10	7	5	5	8	15	20	17	32	32	39	29	25	48	31	17	340

LP316	2016	2017	2018	2019	2020	2021	2022	Total
Jan		2	2	2	2	2	1	11
Feb			1		1	1		3
Mar		1		2	1		2	6
Apr				2		1	3	6
May	1	2	1	2		1	1	8
Jun		1 1	2	7				11
Jul	4R	1 1 1	1	9 3 4	2		1	23
Aug	2	2		3	1 1			10
Sep	2		1	1	2			6
Oct		1		2	25	4	1	33
Nov			1					1
Dec			7	2				9
	9	13	16	39	35	9	9	127

Skomer
North Devon
Camel
Pentire
Porthtowan
West Cornwall East
West Cornwall
St Ives & St Ives Bay
West Penwith North
Mounts Bay
Lizard West

Each seal is unique with a different pattern of movements between a number of sensitive seal sites. Their ID calendars have years across the top and months down the side. The number of IDs at each coloured site shows how much they 'commute' around the coast or not. Left page S112 'Ghost' (top), S89 'Wings' (middle) and S5 'Zigzag' (bottom). Right page S7 'Chairlift' (top), S262 'Ghost 2' (middle) and LP316 'Lucky bunting' (bottom).

became a mature adult, to visiting during the late moulting and early breeding season for a few years. Since 2008 he has very rarely visited after June at all. He surprised us completely in 2016 by turning up right around the coast in Looe and since then he has only put in two appearances on the north cornish coast, completely defecting now and becoming a regular south coast visitor.

Other seals confound us much of the time by making only the occasional visits but even these tell interesting stories. S316 'Triangle Lobster' is a glorious female who commutes between the Isles of Scilly and both coasts of Cornwall, but she was also identified at Sept-Îles in northern France before returning to the Lizard to pup.

The consistency of seasonal seal visits over several years despite changes over time may suggest that seals in Cornwall do have regular seasonal migration routes that they follow according to their life cycle stage. Clearly they know what they are doing, we just need to get better at understanding and thinking seal!

'Zigzag': females are worth fighting over (left)

THINKING LIKE A SEAL...AT WORK, REST AND PLAY

Favourite seal places

As a human, it is hard to assess what makes a good seal haul out site. To really try to understand what a seal is up to, you have to think like a seal. Top priority for a seal must be food, followed by rest, as this is essential for effective digestion. Grey seals are solitary yet social creatures, who appear to seek out the company of other seals for at least part of the year on haul out sites. As a juvenile, interaction is expressed through active play, where seals of both sexes practise the moves they will need for survival into adulthood. For adult seals, company is sought which provides additional security as they sleep and for most females and some males to mate.

Understanding some of a seal's basic needs gives us an insight into the kinds of habitats grey seals must make use of. To complete their lifecycle, grey seals in Cornwall need at least 4 main kinds of habitat:

- **Pupping and breeding habitat:** In Cornwall, seal pups are born on remote, secluded coves or in sea caves made up of either sand and shingle, boulder beaches or both. Some breeding females and males may show breeding site fidelity, returning to the same sites during the breeding season year after year until as a female they are too old to sustain a pregnancy, or as a male they get ousted by a bigger and smarter 'beachmaster'. Other adults show more variability in their breeding season sites.

The best, most established breeding areas must be passed down through generations, but new and more marginal areas may be used if the main site is full to capacity. Recently a popular open beach breeding spot was taken out of action by a major rockfall, blocking access to the seals' favourite alcove under the cliff and completely changing the morphology of the shore. What had been a gently sloping sandy area became a steep boulder slope of sharp-edged un-weathered rocks. It had been a great relief that the rockfall had taken place before the breeding season, albeit only by a week, any later and mothers and pups would almost certainly have been crushed to death.

As the following breeding season developed, the alterations made by the rockfall caused mayhem with the mothers and their pups, as they could no longer access areas above high tide and in big seas at least 2 mothers had to escort their pups round to the adjacent cove and out of sight, to a new area which then became overcrowded.

Whilst we were unable to see the results, the echoing howls of mothers getting in each other's way could frequently be heard from the cliff tops, along with the higher pitched calls of their hungry pups. Most breeding sites are only used during the breeding season and are strangely devoid of any seal activity during the rest of the year. A few breeding sites, probably the more marginal ones, may also function as haul out habitat for seals during the rest of the year.

Since then, two key seal pupping caves have been completely blocked as the entire cliff above them collapsed after the start of the pupping season. An unknown number of mothers and pups would have been trapped and died as a result of this single rockfall, including a favourite seal of mine S14 'Boomers'. Some females returning to the pupping site they haven't visited since last

Breeding caves (left). Breeding habitat: boulder beach (right). Spot the seal!

year may discover their chosen site blocked or already occupied. We assume that in such circumstances a quick change of birthing plan is needed by mum who must be highly adaptable if she and her offspring are to survive. One mum 'Ghost 2' arrived at her usual pupping cave only to find it was already occupied. For the first year ever we observed her and her pup on a different beach a short distance away around the next headland.

• **Haul out habitat:** This is where seals are at their most vulnerable to human disturbance. There are two types of seal haul out sites:

a. **Onshore:** These sites are mostly and often used exclusively during the breeding and moulting seasons and it is here that the largest gatherings of seals can be seen. There are just a sprinkling of these sites in Cornwall and even fewer around the entire southwest coast from Somerset to Dorset.

b. **Offshore:** Gently sloping tidal rocky ledges around offshore islands tend to be used more during the offshore foraging season.

Optimal haul out habitat is hard to pin down, with many sites that look ideal, even those adjacent to established haul out sites remaining unused. Key features probably include more than one access route, so if danger enters via one entrance, the seals can leave through another exit. Entrances must be easily accessible for seals in all sea conditions, so sites must have suitable access ramps at a variety of tidal heights. Protection from the worst of the rough seas is also desirable. Rock skerries or reefs just out to sea help to break up the worst of the waves, giving more shelter to the haul out site.

More exposed offshore islands need suitable leeward sides with protective geomorphology. Deep underwater channels close by may also help seals escape to safety from larger predators such as Orcas (occasionally sighted around the Cornish coast) and humans. Finally, an ability to get out of the prevailing wind reduces the effect of wind chill. These factors combined probably explain why the main onshore seal haul out sites are located on the north Cornish coast and why only smaller seal hauls outs occur on the south coast. Seals are intelligent creatures and will always seek out the most sheltered locations according to human activity, the prevailing wind, sea and weather conditions.

Offshore haul out habitat (right)

Onshore haul out habitats (top and left) and offshore haul out habitat (above)

• **Foraging habitat:** Least is known about this aspect of grey seal habitat in Cornwall, although ideas can be gathered from what is known about seal diet and diving behaviour. Grey seals are opportunistic bottom feeders and are thought to nuzzle around the seabed which they proactively search with their whiskers, aiming to disturb sand eels and dragonets, which they snap up 'down in one' as they emerge from the sand. Sand eels are the preferred food of grey seals which make up the bulk of their diet, although seals are generalist feeders and do eat a wide variety of fish species, particularly benthic species and gadoids. Foraging habitat must be linked to large areas of sand and gravel substrates that form sand eel habitat. Knowing that seals dive on average to 60 metres for pelagic dives and 120m for benthic trips begins to delimit key foraging areas, although one female grey seal was recorded diving to an incredible 455 metres!

• **Transit habitat:** As seals move around the Cornish coast and beyond to the Celtic fringe, they need safe and quieter transit routes linking up all the other 3 types of seal habitat. Whether these routes are narrow seal motorways linking up haul out service stations or are generalised 'freedom to roam'

areas of sea is something we have yet to discover.

Understanding the connectivity of grey seal habitat by individual seal functional movements revealed by photo ID and the interface with seal seasons is essential for the effective future conservation of this charismatic mobile marine mammal species. Interestingly, many areas of coast favoured by seals for hauling out across Cornwall and the rest of England are owned by the National Trust, in whose care seals thrive. Working with landowners of haul out habitat is critical for the survival of a species upon which diversified coastal economic prosperity depends.

Offshore foraging habitat

VARIED BEHAVIOURS

A quick glance at a seal haul out site may give the impression of passive inactivity, with most seals sleeping soundly. Careful observation over even a short period of time can reveal a wide range of varied and often amusing behaviours. Detailed knowledge of individual seals often exposes the fluid nature of a haul out, as seals who one minute are sleeping have a quick scrap and then disappear into the sea, only to return a few minutes later, wander around the haul out, annoying other

Seal swimming (above) and offshore female (right)

seals before finding the perfect spot and falling asleep again. Take your eye off a seal haul out and within minutes, it is all change – a bit like only opening your eyes when the participants are sitting down during a game of musical chairs!

Haul out sites are in a constant state of flux with continually rising and receding tides. As the tide goes out seals may spread out over a greater area of beach, track down the beach to keep close to the water's edge or, if spooked by a loud voice or bark from the clifftop, suddenly realise they are a long way from the tide line and stampede at speed to get nearer the safety of the sea. Close inspection with superzoom lenses shows stampeding seals invariably leave blood trails as they rush over sharp rocks, shells or things left behind by people such as nails sticking out of wood.

Seals tend to be more active on a rising tide as they are forced into a smaller area, thus routinely invading other seals' personal space. They will spin round to move away from the water, flipper politely at seals in front of them to request access or barge their way through the crowd if their appeals are ignored. Whilst surrounding seals may posture their

displeasure at this, they all understand what is going on, and so tolerate intruders more affably. This is the best and most entertaining time to watch seals.

Behaviours are best categorised according to where the seals are – in the sea, on land or moving between the two.

Sea based behaviours

• **Swimming:** Seals move gracefully through the water propelled by sideways movements of alternately fanned rear flippers. Seals can, of course, swim from a still beach start, a seal can attain a very fast speed in just a few seconds doing handbrake turns repeatedly. Our partnership photo ID work with The Seal Project proves that BRX4 'Square Eyes' swam from the Camel Estuary to South Devon in just 3 days – a journey of nearly 300 kilometres.

• **Bottling:** Sleeping vertically in the sea with their nose poking through the surface, seals may resemble a floating bottle. Seals breathe erratically and will open their nostrils a few times and then breath-hold. Seals can sink vertically during their sleep and when carbon dioxide levels rise in their blood; a reflex in their rear flippers causes a twitch which

Seal bottling

returns the seal to the surface. Seals may bottle in the same location for some time or may intersperse bottling with repeated diving cycles in time and space, when seals have been observed to sleep in a chosen place lying on the seabed.

• **Logging:** Alternatively, seals may sleep horizontally at the surface of the sea. This can be one of the most worrying behaviours to watch, as a seal has the appearance of being dead and only gives themself away when they scull with their flippers or very slightly raise their nostrils clear of the water to breathe. The seals most likely to 'log' at the surface are moulted pups under a year old which seem to prefer logging to bottling and this naturally adds to the level of concern.

Seal diving

Seal snorkelling

• **Eating:** Surprisingly, this is a relatively rare sight. Most seal food goes down in one and an underwater video taken by Dave McBride shows pregnant females foraging at depth on a wreck surrounded by small herring. As a fish vibration is felt close to a whisker, the female telescopes her neck to snatch and grab the herring and with no further jaw movements the fish is unceremoniously sucked into her mouth and disappears. Larger prey cannot be swallowed whole, so must be taken to the surface to be broken into pieces before eating. Only the central part of the fish may be held in the mouth as the seal shakes its head violently to break the fish apart. The seal will allow broken chunks of fish to sink and then dive down to retrieve them

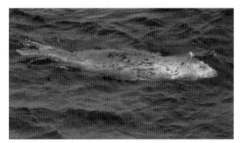
Seal logging

and repeat until the whole fish has gone. Alternatively, the seal may hold the fish in its fore flippers as it treads water at the surface and bites chunks out of the fish. As a seal's fore flipper digits are not very dexterous, they don't make great fish clamps, especially when a lot of tugging is involved.

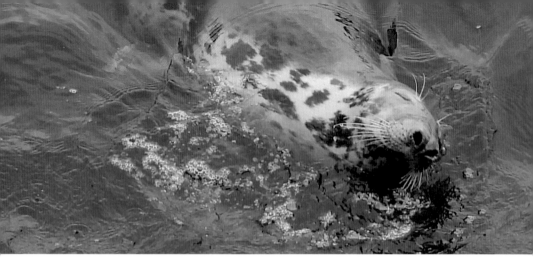

'Crosscomb' in a sleep cycle

- **Diving:** Seals usually dive head first, having blown most of the air from their lungs and using their rear flippers to power them downwards. It is always amusing to see white-coat pups trying to dive against their natural buoyancy, which usually leaves their rear flippers splashing about at the surface. Only when their lower abdominal muscles grow strong enough will they be able to generate enough propulsion to counteract their buoyancy. One-week-old pups have been seen successfully diving underwater, but they soon 'bob' back up to the surface! Seals have been seen to go underwater and then let out bubbles of air which rise to, and burst at the surface, breaking in rings that ripple out concentrically confusing any onlooker who turned too late to see the seal. In these cases, the seal must have premeditated the action, by holding a small amount of air in its mouth, which it later released underwater. This is a favourite behaviour of female S161 'Crosscomb' who has blown bubble rings since she was a juvenile.

- **Snorkelling:** Seals that are relaxed and resting at the surface may position their nostrils half in and half out of the water. As air is exhaled from their lungs explosively, it creates bubbles which accompany the seal's audible snorts. Occasionally seals may be heard before they are seen and may be given away by their loud snorting, but this tends to be an adult behaviour!

Some offshore water-based behaviours are more social and involve more than one seal:

• **Dancing:** This graceful and acrobatic behaviour is a real treat to watch. Two or more seals may swim around each other, sometimes in spirals in very close proximity. Occasionally, seals are seen performing synchronised swimming movements worth a 9.5 on anyone's scoring system!

Beachmaster (top) and wannabe squaring up for a fight

• **Splashing:** Using a fore flipper to create a splash at the surface is a common attention seeking behaviour. In contrast, seals may also splash to deter unwanted attention when another seal or person is too close to them in the water. Interestingly, this behaviour is sometimes used to gain human attention, particularly in harbours where seals beg for food. Please always resist the temptation to feed wild seals as, for reasons explained later in the **Threats** section of this book, it has lifelong damaging impacts on both seals and humans.

• **Fighting:** Aggressive fights are rare and usually only occur during the breeding season. Much of a fight involves posturing as a usual precursor to the main event. If signals are read well, the fight may never take place, but if evenly matched, a fight may ensue. A particularly fierce encounter that took place off a key breeding site involved a lot of loud snarling and splashing. Whilst it was difficult to see the precise details of what was going on, the seals were aiming to bite their opponent's necks and once gripped would shake their heads as roughly as possible. As both seals tire, there is some sort of nonverbal agreement to rest stationary for a short while before re-starting. In Cornwall fights don't often last long, as it soon becomes clear who is the strongest, bravest seal and the pretender quickly gives in. Pretenders usually reverse back whilst facing the 'winner' as turning tail too quickly could risk injury to a delicate and precious rear flipper. The funniest aspect of these serious contests is the effect they have on the other seals hauled out in the area, who react rather like children in a school playground, all rushing to gather around the fight. In this way, perhaps a 'beachmaster's' reputation is strengthened, as some younger males will not bother to challenge the 'beachmaster', having witnessed how he dealt with bigger and stronger seals!

crash dive again, but may react with curiosity and explore the stimulus from a different position a few metres away.

• **Tracking:** People at sea in slow moving human powered vessels are a constant source of amusement for seals. Although hauled seals are often wary of silent craft that sneak up on them too close, seals in the sea may choose to observe this potential threat from a safe distance and usually from behind. As a result, the seal effectively tracks the vessel looking at it for a few seconds and then swimming underwater to keep up with it. As the seal often snorts just before it dives,

• **Crash diving:** Seals that are spooked and scared at sea by something or someone will crash dive very suddenly, causing a great splash visually and audibly. This instant reaction will be followed by the uncertain seal returning to the surface a short distance away to take another look at what spooked them. If they remain scared, they will

Crash-diving and periscoping due to disturbance

this causes the vessel's puzzled occupant/s to look round. It is almost as if the seal waits until they have looked away again before returning to the surface for another good look.

Land based behaviours

• **Sleeping:** Seals may sleep in a variety of positions on the beach. Many just lie on their bellies, falling asleep the moment their head touches the sand, although they remain vigilant and keep looking up on regular occasions; vigilance becoming less active as the seal settles down and is reassured about its safety. Other seals prefer to sleep on their sides and some seals may have a preferred side to sleep on. Very relaxed seals who have been out of the sea for a longer period of time, will lie on their backs, exposing their bellies. They curl their rear flippers round each other and their tail in a cute fashion, presumably to prevent heat loss and keep sensitive bits warm!

• **Stretching and yawning:** Sleep is regularly broken up with rear flipper fanning and whole body stretches. These reveal just how flexible seals are, as it is perfectly possible for a seal to arc its body so far that its nose virtually touches its rear flippers. Yawns tend to be

Seals sleeping (top); pillow-talk (above)

great gaping affairs, accompanied by rolling their heads back and round in a circle, which

Stretching (above left); yawning (above right), and head rubbing (left)

exaggerates the usually silent yawn. A yawn is often followed by some open mouthed tongue licks.

• **Head rubbing:** This activity often accompanies yawning. A seal will use a partly fanned out fore flipper to wipe over the top or side of its head and face, in an action that appears to be very satisfying to the seal.

• **Hauling:** The hauling action of a seal has been described previously, but it is worth noting that, over a sandy beach, seals leave distinctive haul trails. A single central drag line slightly narrower than the seal's body has paired fore flipper prints either side of it, sometimes with sand thrown up in front of the print in the same direction as the seal was moving. The speed that the seal was moving corresponds to the distance between these prints. Prints close together are made by a relaxed, slow moving seal, whereas prints which are far apart tell you that the seal was moving at speed. One of the few times a seal's tail is held straight upwards is when the seal is hauling over shingle or boulders. As a seal leaves the water it goes through a range of body shaking (like a dog spraying water from its fur), stretching, yawning and face rubbing which are repeated until the seal is ready to sleep.

• **Scratching:** This is a common activity for hauled out seals, particularly during the moulting season when seals seem to be at their most sensitive. As with humans, most itches are accessible, but it is the ones on their backs that pose the greatest challenge! An irresistible back itch that just has to be scratched results in the most amusing of all seal behaviours – the breakdance! The seal is forced to writhe in 3 dimensions that often results in the seal moving sideways across the beach.

• **Bananaing:** This behaviour has been described elsewhere in this book. It is the reaction of a dry seal to being showered or washed over by the surf, often on a rising tide. As seals tend to prefer lying close to the edge of the sea, their position must change as the tide goes out and comes in. As a result it

Seal on the move (top), haul trail of pup (centre) and scratching breakdance (bottom)

is not unusual for groups of seals to be seen bananaing together. A seal's body is covered with insulating blubber, all apart from its extremities – flippers and head. As the cold water washes over their super sensitive bits, the seal will bend and use muscle tension to raise them above the cold water. The banana behaviour is repeated with each incoming wave, until the seal finally decides either to go into the sea, or to move further up the beach, where the behaviour will have to be repeated a short while later. Should the seal decide to return to the sea, it will tolerate its body being covered in water, followed by its rear flippers, but sometimes a seal can be seen swimming out to sea with a completely dry head above the water, as if it simply can't bear the cold and will only dive at the last possible minute.

• **Digging and sand snuffling:** This is one of the rarer seal behaviours. Young seals in particular can be seen using their snouts to dig down or snuffle into the sand, apparently following a scent, possibly of a previous seal or the behaviour may be linked to feeding actions on the sea bed. An alternative theory is that every beach has a different scent to a seal arising from its unique bacterial composition. It is possible that a seal can tell exactly

which beach it is on by its smell. Young seals unfamiliar with the beach, may sand snuffle to deeply engage with the scent in order to learn it and commit it to memory for future reference. Sometimes a seal will progress to digging with its fore flippers alternately in an

Sand snuffling (top) and a big strong alpha male (above)

action that resembles a turtle. Other times, seals arriving on a beach will deliberately roll repeatedly as if to cover themselves in sand and perhaps the pleasantly familiar smell of the beach. Of course, they may be doing this to mask their presence using aural or visual camouflage.

Some land based behaviours are more social and involve more than one seal

• **Prone howling:** This is a behaviour that appears to be limited to juvenile males as they become adults. Apparently wild with rampaging hormones, these poor adolescent males give the impression of being in unbearable pain. Their howling is often the first aspect of this behaviour to be noticed. The afflicted youngster will be rolling around the beach and stretching his body lengthways until he resembles a thin sausage. He will then extend his telescopic neck and press it down onto the sand before opening his mouth and emitting long slow piercing howls. Whilst this whole melodrama looks very worrying and may last a considerable time, the perpetrator usually stops quite suddenly and resumes normal service as if nothing has happened.

• **Body slapping:** Often in conjunction with prone howling, a few juveniles, as well as adult males have been observed deliberately lifting their bodies up from wet sand and slamming them back down, in order to make a loud slapping noise accompanied by a big splash. This behaviour is thought to be attention seeking, as if to say, 'look at me! I'm a big, strong seal!' Science has shown that bigger seals are able to send out ripples of vibrations to other seals over 100m away through sandy substrate. Body slapping may be repeated a few times followed by a bit of threatening behaviour.

• **Princess behaviour or flirting:** Young females coming into season for the first time spend a lot of their time trying to attract male attention. They will pester sleeping males by repeatedly approaching and sniffing them and resorting to howling and flippering at them if they get no reaction. When the sleepy male finally wakes up and takes an interest, she will shoot down towards the water in a provocative manner, returning to irritate him if he needs reminding she is there. In extreme cases, the young female will shake her head wildly from side to side and rush around the beach in a crazy fashion to get everyone's attention.

On one occasion, a young female seal called 'Spade' was showing off to a group of males who were studiously ignoring her. Unbeknown to 'Spade' she had gained the attention of a very large old male further along the beach called 'Teddy'. 'Teddy' dragged himself out of his slumber and hauled across to where 'Spade' was tormenting the group of younger males. He cautiously approached her and began sniffing her. 'Spade' immediately looked horrified at the appearance of her new suitor and seemed to shrink in size before our very eyes, apparently hoping for a hole in the sand to swallow her up. She tried to escape but 'Teddy' followed on behind. Fortunately, 'Teddy' was a wise old seal and somewhat of a gentleman! He soon got the message and returned to his slumber, leaving 'Spade' a little shaken, and hopefully a little less wanton!

- **Sniffing:** Most seals say hello to each other with a 'sniff greeting'. One seal will either sniff the nose/mouth of the second seal or more often around the ear hole. The behaviour is usually reciprocated by the other seal. Sometimes a seal will sniff and hardly cause a reaction and both seals will settle down or move on. Other times, a recoil reaction is observed, perhaps as the seals fail to recognise one another, or recognise each other as a foe. One seal may then leave or both may growl, or snarl, posture, perhaps even fight or chase each other down the beach and into the sea. Pups that have become separated from their mums by stormy seas will approach other seals on the beach in their desperate search for their mother and a feed. Females turning round to sniff them will appear to dislike the smell and retreat away from the pup. Males and juveniles know pups mean trouble, so move away too. Pups can be persistent and repeatedly try to suckle from other seals – from other pups to adult males. They are tolerated to begin with, but will respond with increasing levels of threat. Having said this looks can be deceiving!

Seals playing

Sniff greeting (opposite top and bottom left), lucky male sniff-greeted by two females (opposite bottom right)

I watched a separated pup called 'Maple' spend 10 minutes trying to suckle an adult male. At first he moved away, then turned round to growl, then snapped and eventually put the whole of the pup's head inside his mouth. I was horrified when the pup was released to see pink on the top of the desperate pup's head. I had already called a rescue, but the British Divers Marine Life Medic team had not fully arrived. When the pup was finally rescued successfully and thoroughly checked by the animal care team at the Cornish Seal Sanctuary 'Maple' had no puncture wounds at all on her head. So the pink must have been bloody saliva and the head clamp as serious a warning as any pup was ever going to get without being injured. Many species have an innate respect for infants and have developed harmless 'child care' strategies - it seems seals have too!

Starving pups moving round a lot to search for their mums wear bald sore patches under their fore flippers not yet tough enough for so much activity. Pups try to suckle anything from sands, to rocks and limpets. This leads to worn sore patches under their chins. Raw pink skin under a pups fore flippers and chin are red flags that the pup is in trouble and has lost its mum.

'Rocket's' mother, who was blind in one eye, once mistakenly approached the wrong pup as she returned from the sea to feed 'Rocket'. Her first sniff of the pup resulted in a recoil action as she realised this was not her pup and she hurriedly turned and moved away in search of her own.

- **Flippering:** Seals usually like to have their own socially distanced personal space,

Starving pup trying to suckle from feeding pup

Seals playing

only occasionally tolerating ongoing physical contact with other seals. Adult females can be particularly vociferous about this and will howl towards the invader of their personal space. If this doesn't work, she will turn around and swat the offending seal repeatedly with her fore flipper. Occasionally this doesn't work either and then, interestingly and somewhat surprisingly, both seals may just go to sleep, either in close proximity or touching each other. Apparently neither seal being willing to give ground or lose face!

- **Playing:** Young seals seem to love playing and will do so for hours on end. Two or more of them will roll around each other in the shallows, or chase each other across the beach, waking up all the adults in an annoying fashion! Photo identification shows that two seals may end up playing around for days on end, either with the same seal or with a different partner. Sometimes playing groups are all male, or male and female, but it is almost unheard of to see two females of any age playing together. Occasionally the adults object to being woken up and will split the playing juveniles up, but once the air is clear and it has all calmed down, the playing individuals will often reunite and resume their games. Whilst less active, it is

Rolling pinning

not unusual to see adult males playing kindly with each other. Maybe they are happy to have re-united with a friend of old and are repeating behaviour they once did, albeit with less energy and agility.

• **Rolling pinning:** A particularly popular playing manoeuvre for juvenile seals is the 'rolling pin'. Here one seal positions itself at right angles midway to its partner's back before launching itself over the top of its partner and pinning them to the sand. Once their fore flippers are splayed wide across the partner's back for balance, the pinned seal can be rolled back and forth in play. This is not usually tolerated for long, but looks good fun!

• **Chasing:** Seals of all ages may chase each other around the beach for numerous reasons ranging from fun through to aggression. Seals that move very quickly across the beach are great to watch and youngsters may give the impression of bouncing along due to the favourable power to weight ratios, whilst older seals can lumber at best.

• **Rolling:** This is a highly submissive behaviour, most frequently used by dominant adult males to show they are not a threat.

'Beachmasters' regularly check out the females on their patch, sniffing them, presumably as a test to see if they are ready to mate. Once the female makes it clear she is not ready, by howling and flippering him, he will retreat, beginning with a submissive roll or two to get away from her.

• **Threatening:** It is easy to tell when a seal is being threatening. Its open-mouthed stance, bearing full sets of visibly sharp, interlocking teeth and the deep snarling growls of males or higher pitched howls of females are unmistakeable. A rule of thumb for people working in seal rehabilitation centres is not to go within a broom handle's length of a seal. The reason being that seals have elastic, telescopic necks that can lunge and instantaneously stretch to the length of a broom handle to bite you! The same is true on the beach, with seals lunging at each other to force the other to retreat. Usually this is clever, fine-tuned posturing with distances carefully judged to avoid direct physical contact. But accidents happen and arc-shaped bite marks can be inflicted.

• **Fighting:** As opposed to threatening, fighting is clearly much more serious and aggressive and involving more physical

Threatening behaviour

Males sparring

contact. Juvenile seals will play fight and adult females will strongly threaten to protect their pups, but usually it is only adult males who will fight. Aggressors will aim to move to lie next to each other side by side in order to gain ground to lunge at, bite and grip their opponent's neck. Bites during fighting will pull the skin away from the blubber layer and may result in chunks of flesh being ripped out, so fights can be a bloody affair. Fighting males seem oblivious to everything around them, causing other seals to scatter or injuring innocent bystanders. When a 'beachmaster' is a strong leader, fighting is rare, often a look from the 'beachmaster' is enough to scare all but the most evenly matched seals off his patch. Even well-matched males rarely fight for long, one soon realising that discretion is the better part of valour.

• **Stampeding:** In a relaxed haul out, seals will lie facing in all directions randomly across the beach. A haul out that has been recently disturbed is characterised by seals all lining up to face the sea. Stampedes are always shocking as they begin so suddenly. Just one scared seal can trigger a stampede. As it bolts towards the sea, it sets up a domino reaction throughout the haul out and in no time at all, increasing numbers of seals are heading seawards. Stampedes are often quite loud, as pebbles and rocks are moved by the rushing seals. If the wind is blowing towards you, a stampede can be smelt too. Seals have a very sour musky smell and their rapid movement releases odours that carry in the wind. Carelessly rushing over rocks can cause linear cuts to bellies and fore flippers or ripped out claws caught between boulders.

- **Emerging from the sea:** A seal arriving at a haul out will often practice a ritualistic routine of behaviour. As the seal enters the shallows to a beach or the white water around an island, it will look vigilantly at the haul out to search for the presence of other seals and to get a feel for the movement of the water in the area. If other seals are present and the situation safe, the seal will begin to emerge from the sea. Once clear of the water, the seal will sometimes shake its head, spraying water everywhere – presumably to clear its ears of water and then look around warily. Active nostrils reveal the seal to be sniffing the air carefully too, aiming to sense danger. If unsure, the seal may return to the sea, only to repeat the activity a few minutes later.

The newly hauled seal will cautiously approach the nearest group of hauled seals and sniff one of them, who invariably jumps a mile and turns to growl its disapproval for such a rude and sudden awakening. Should the newly hauled seal settle too close and in the personal space of another seal, it will be repeatedly swatted by the fore flipper of the established seal, as well as being howled at to say 'get out of my face!' Once it is sure it is safe to do so, the new arrival will find a suitable and comfortable spot and start

'Beachmaster' fighting a challenger (top), disturbed seals stampeding to the safety of the sea (bottom)

to snooze, but will wake up frequently to perform a visual check of its surroundings before settling back to sleep.

• **Returning to the sea:** The manner in which a seal returns to the sea depends on its location in relation to the sea and its mood. Some appear to make a sudden decision to head seawards, others will resist the inevitable for as long as they can before finally taking the plunge. Occasionally seals that have hauled out at high tide get marooned well above the waterline when they re-awake at low tide.

These seals occasionally panic, when a route back to the sea is not obvious or involves a steep drop. High dives have been known, as have earth shattering 'tombstone' belly flops as seals land in shallow rock pools, which can be very distressing to witness. It is critically important that we stay well away from any seal hauled high above the water line to avoid risk of injury. Other seals will become increasingly wet as the tide rises over them and may even use their claws and body friction to hang on as long as possible. For those on offshore rock skerries in a calm sea, the seals may even appear to be resting on the water surface, as a rising tide encroaches,

only to be floated off when their buoyancy can be resisted no longer.

Male seal sleeping (above), juvenile tombstoning into sea risks life threatening injury (bottom)

SEAL STORIES

'Chairlift': *'Chairlift' is a very special seal and one of my very favourites! He was the first seal to be added to my photo identification catalogue back in June 2000. He is named after a pattern on the right side of his neck, which to me looks like a button ski lift, that no-one else seems able to 'see'! Needless to say, I get a lot of stick for 'Chairlift's' name. When I first met 'Chairlift', he was probably around 2 or 3 years old and a bit girly looking! I have had the unrivalled privilege of watching him grow up in his natural environment. As a juvenile, 'Chairlift' loved playing in the shallows with other seals.*

'Chairlift' yawning

As he hit adolescence, he spent hours play fighting with other male seals of a similar age, such as 'Lighthouse' and '23' but this resembled handbags at dawn and he has been known to fall asleep mid bout, with his head resting on his opponent's neck, only to resume sparring again when both of them are woken from their snooze. 'Chairlift' was the first seal that I saw over 100 times and I have now identified him 344 times over 22 different years.

Most of his visits were during the moulting and breeding seasons, but as he hit the age of 10 or 11, he visited less frequently during the breeding season. In 2010, we were very excited to find he had been photographed on the Island of Skomer by the South and West Wales Wildlife Trust attempting to 'beachmaster'. This appears to have been a one off visit and perhaps an unsuccessful attempt at mating. Only one other time has 'Chairlift' been identified anywhere other than the West Cornwall site – in Oct 2014, we saw him at the West Penwith North site.

As he's aged, he has visited West Cornwall less frequently. I've watched him in a variety of locations and whilst he loves sleeping and rolling his head round in exaggerated yawns, he is also a very active seal, although I have never seen him being aggressive towards other seals, despite the fact he is now a mature adult in the prime of his life. For seals that don't get to pass on their genes, perhaps this is their lot— 'Chairlift' seems to be a very contented seal and if it is possible, he is a seal with a very kindly face and no breeding mane or at least, not one covered with battle scars! He spends his time swimming, eating and sleeping. Lucky seal.

'Wriggle': Out of all the pups I have observed over the years, 'Wriggle's' first delighted me the most! She is a beautiful adult female seal, although she has a very distinctive scar above her right eye, that gives her a constantly surprised look on one side! She chose to have

'Wriggle'

her first pup in a good viewing spot and she had the most gorgeous looking fluffy pup that we called 'Bubbles'. I began watching Bubble's development from day one and was able to see her first feed.

I was quite anxious when a week later, 'Wriggle' decided to take 'Bubbles' for a swim. During a feed, 'Wriggle' moved her body and hauled down to the water's edge, forcing her hungry pup to follow. As soon as her pup latched on again, 'Wriggle' moved into the water and 'Bubbles' followed only to be rolled over by the small breakers. It was an anxious time, but 'Wriggle' kept very close to her pup. 'Bubbles' didn't know she could put her head underwater, so 'Wriggle' had to gently nudge her underwater for the first time. As 'Bubbles' got the hang of swimming, she and Mum had some very tender moments together, appearing to kiss nose to nose on several occasions. After a short while, Mum decided to bring 'Bubbles' back to shore, but they got separated by a very large wave. 'Wriggle' could be seen raising her head clear of the water to search for her pup who she found safe and sound and then both returned to the beach to resume the feed!

A week later, it was all change. 'Bubbles' no longer wanted to get wet and when Mum tried the same trick, 'Bubbles' refused to follow! In fact, this time, 'Bubbles' forced Mum to follow her further and further up the beach to feed. As soon as 'Bubbles' latched on, we could see the reason why, as a big wave lapped right behind 'Bubble's' rear flippers. Even at such a young age, it seemed 'Bubbles' had an instinctive knowledge about how far up the beach the next wave would reach. 'Wriggle' weaned her pup on the maximum lactation period of 21 days, after which both of them disappeared from the cove.

Despite being seen, 'Wriggle' didn't pup again for another four years. That October she was photographed by Dave McBride on the Isles of Scilly looking sufficiently fat to be pregnant. By October, 'Wriggle' was back in Cornwall and in early October she gave birth to her second pup, 'Seaspray'. It was interesting to learn that as a breeding female, 'Wriggle' had arrived from a westerly direction to pup on the north Cornish coast. 'Wriggle' had a season off and then lost her third pup 'Limestone' the following year. With disbelief that it was even possible, we watched a distraught 'Wriggle' climb up a huge cuboid boulder so she could scan the boulder beach in search of her missing pup. It was heart-breaking for us...and perhaps for her, as a few months after this she disappeared off our radar. It is always sad to lose a friend, but her memory will live long in our hearts.

'Ghost 2': Early one September, Rob Jutsum was taking a short break in north Devon and he took some photos of a small collection of seals hauled out on rock ledges. Interested to learn more, his photos were sent to Devon Biodiversity Records Centre, who forwarded them on to me, as Rob had asked questions about one seal in particular. Immediately on seeing the photo, I realised I knew the female, as she had had her pup in West Cornwall on the north Cornish coast the year before. Females who pup here may not be seen during the moulting and foraging seasons, so it has always been a mystery where they spend the rest of their year. I waited in anticipation at my local patch for 'Ghost 2' to turn up and was delighted and amazed when 12 days later she appeared right on cue looking heavily pregnant and had her pup 3 days after that. 'Ghost 2' had been hauled out on spiky rocks in north Devon, having completed a journey of over 140 kilometres carrying her pup, only to haul out over another boulder beach exhausted and about to pup. She successfully fed and weaned this pup, named 'Rocky', inspired by his location. This despite him getting into endless scrapes – trapped between boulders, sneaking behind his Mum's back into big breakers and ending up on a different part of the beach altogether!

Since this momentous occasion, 'Ghost 2' has returned 12 times from north Devon to have her pup in Cornwall over 15 years. She gives birth inside a cave accessed via a small vertical slit in the cliffs. Our seal mums really are incredibly resilient. 'Ghost 2' has coped with several cliff collapses blocking her cave and recently had to change pupping beaches completely when her favourite cave was already occupied on her arrival from north Devon. After learning that 'Wriggle' had swum in to pup from the west, it was interesting to know that 'Ghost 2' had arrived from the opposite direction!

A pregnant 'Ghost 2', three days before giving birth to her pup (top), mating at sea (middle); 'Beachmaster' 'W' has a distinctive scar on his thigh mating on land (bottom)

'Beachmaster' 'W': *The first mating seal I ever photographed back in 2002 was 'W' – only identifiable from a small W shaped scar down on his right thigh. I hadn't recognised 'W' at the time, but did so 3 years later, a year after he had become the established dominant male or 'beachmaster' on the West Cornwall breeding beach. 'W' was not the largest male seal on the beach, in fact he had few distinctive features. Yet somehow, he was able to stamp his authority across the breeding beach with just one look. He reigned supreme for 5 years, only having one really serious scrap which left a slight scar on the top of his back. He took his 'beachmaster' duties very seriously once there were 2 pups on the breeding beach – it seems mating with only one female wasn't worth exerting his energy for!*

The sixth year however, despite arriving in September at the start of the breeding season, he disappeared after less than a week and we feared he had been ousted by a younger and stronger adult male. From that point on, there were a series of new 'beachmasters', each lasting just a few days. The lack of strong leadership on the breeding beach caused anarchy, with males regularly scrapping with each other, disturbing all the other seals. How we longed for the return of 'W'. We hadn't realised what a strong and calming influence he'd had on the others.

Much to our relief 'W' returned at the end of November. He looked fit and well, but was a shadow of his former self. He skulked up the beach under the camouflage of the cliff, only moving when the incumbent 'beachmaster' wasn't looking. It was a bit like playing the children's game 'Statues'; 'W' would freeze every time the reigning 'beachmaster' turned to face him. 'W' got about half way up the beach, but the moment 'W' and the 'beachmaster' made eye contact from over 100 metres, 'W' was off, hurtling back to the sea. 'W' had lost his confidence and with it whatever 'x' factor he has possessed and with it his control of the breeding beach. We hope he will enjoy his retirement and achieve the level of contentment exhibited by non breeding males like 'Chairlift'.

'Medallion Man': *A young adult male seal, 'Medallion Man' was first identified at a wild seal haul out at around the age of 4. Since then, however, he has developed a taste for life in harbours – Newquay Harbour to be specific. Seals are intelligent creatures and 'Medallion Man' is one of those seals who through a quirk of fate learned of the easy pickings that can be had around active fishing harbours. Fish discards probably lure seals into harbours in the first place.*

People on trip boats are always delighted to see seals and those that have been out on leisure fishing cruises themselves can often be persuaded to part with a few fish on their return to the harbour and so begins a life of habituated, humanised, stressed behaviour that is likely to last the seal's lifetime. Seals who spend any time in harbours are exposed to a whole new range of threats ranging from the superficial – algal growth on their backs to the much more serious and potentially life threatening – propeller wounds, getting hooked in anglers line or the ingestion and inhalation of diesel fuel.

'Medallion Man'

Fortunately, 'Medallion Man' only spends a short amount of time hanging around Newquay harbour before returning to the wild seal haul outs. During one TV filming trip we did with Jodie Kidd for Country Tracks, 'Medallion Man' turned up at the side of our boat. Jodie and I simultaneously leant over and greeted him with a 'Hello gorgeous' in stereo! There are not many celebrity seals who have been described as gorgeous by a human supermodel!

We were hoping that he wouldn't follow the example of another seal, 'Superman', who spent 4 years commuting between Newquay Harbour and the wild seal haul outs before disappearing never to be seen again.

It seems our fears materialised. 'Medallion Man' is one of many young adult male seals who died in his early teenage prime years. We are not sure why, but speculate that marine pollutants such as PCBs might be to blame. These toxins, although now banned, persist in the marine environment and accumulate in body fats. Females are able to offload their toxins to their first-born pup (pretty much condemning it to death), but thereafter their lower toxic burdens enable them and the future offspring to survive. Males have no offload mechanism and too many of them have died for this to be a coincidence.

'Puffa' - the rehabilitated seal: *'Puffa' was rescued from Sennen Cove at the age of a week and a half and still with her white coat, despite being well fed and fat. On high Spring tides and rough seas, 'Puffa' may have been washed out of her birthing site and away from her Mum. As 'Puffa' had been handled by humans who were trying to be helpful, the Seal Sanctuary Animal Care Team had little choice but to rescue her from a beach that had a lot of human activity. During her clinical assessment it was discovered that 'Puffa' had an infected nail bed, so she was given antibiotics and the middle claw on her right fore flipper was removed. After a successful convalescence and reintegration with the resident adult seals at Gweek, 'Puffa' was released within six months at Gunwalloe. 21 months later, 'Puffa' was identified at a north coast haul out where the yellow flipper tag 079 on her right rear flipper was photographed.*

A regular visitor to this site, 'Puffa' has been seen every year since.

At the age of 5, 'Puffa' was looking heavily pregnant, although she must have had her pup in a sensibly secret location. The following year, 'Puffa' gave birth at an open beach site, and whilst her birth wasn't seen, it was heard, alerting everyone to the new arrival – a very bemused looking pup we called 'Puffling'. It has been wonderful to watch a rehabilitated seal behaving like all the other wild seals and breeding success is the ultimate indicator of this, strengthening 'Puffa's' place as a firm favourite with Seal Sanctuary staff and Cornwall Seal Group Research Trust supporters alike. 'Puffa' is now 17 years old and still going strong...long may this continue.

'Puffa', aged 5 years and 2 months (opposite)

THREATS TO GREY SEALS IN CORNWALL AND WHAT WE CAN DO TO HELP THEM

Juvenile caught in human toy flying ring

Global biodiversity loss has occurred across terrestrial, aquatic and atmospheric biomes as a result of human driven overexploitation, habitat destruction, invasive species, pollution and climate change. These impact cumulatively on essential ecosystem functioning upon which human society depends.

Survival in the open ocean and around our coast is tough and even helpless looking seal pups must be born hardy. Huge storms whip our seas into tumultuous peaks and deep abysses. Breakers relentlessly pound our shores energised by gigantic Atlantic swells sometimes for weeks on end. Low tides provide some respite, but at high tide most seals are forced to take their chances at sea. Small pups with muscles still to develop, can tire quickly and on quiet days after a lengthy winter storm, many calls are made to the British Divers Marine Life Rescue 24 hour hotline by members of the public concerned about white coated or moulted pups they have seen.

Each call is followed up and pups are often found with broken limbs, jaws, ribs and

'Splash' surrounded by plastic bottles

smashed skulls. Such is the harshness of their natural environment. With climate change leading to ever increasingly frequent extreme weather events, this looks set to continue. I am left asking the question...what is 'natural' these days as our planetary impact reaches to the top of our atmosphere and into our deepest ocean spaces.

Most frustrating are the seals that are found with avoidable conditions often because of human interaction. One of the most gruesome photographs I received was of a juvenile seal with an open wound down half of the left side of its face thought to have been caused by a boat strike. I have photographed another adult female with the right half of her face caved into a right angle after a similar collision. Being out at sea is risky, so we need to look after ourselves, consider the marine life we share our oceans with and take suitable care.

Marine litter can be found on any beach in varying quantities, but the beach morphology will inevitably accumulate more rubbish in some areas than others, sometimes trapping it for months on end. As playful and curious creatures, seals are unable to resist exploring

Entangled juveniles in monofilament (left) and trawl net (middle). 'Legs' in desperate need of rescue (right

something unusual in the water and have been seen eating floating crisp packets and dragging durable plastic sacks underwater, only to surface in a panic, as the plastic has broken leaving a piece trapped round a tooth. Worse still, a beautiful white coated seal pup swam headfirst into a see-through plastic bag floating just beneath the surface. Seals are erratic breathers, so at first this merely presented a challenge against which to swim, but as the pup returned to the surface and tried to take its first breath, its panic was visible. After a few seconds, the pup had the intelligence to reverse and was fortunate to lose its suffocating mask.

'Splash' was one of few white coated pups that I have watched, who loved going in the sea almost from birth. He would be seen swimming just offshore and always with his Mum, 'Waves',

in close attendance on most days and his pleasure was obvious to see. But during one particularly high tide, I had to endure watching 'Splash' struggling to keep afloat at the back of his birthing zawn with his mother anxiously trying to protect him by using her body to break up the worst of the waves on the seaward side of him.

As 'Splash' was tumbled by the 'washing machine' effect of the sea, he was repeatedly hit by plastic bottles, an oil drum and a large plank of wood that had all been funnelled up by the force of the water into 'Splash's' zawn. This was such a distressing experience, as at the time I had no idea whether 'Splash' would survive his battering or not. Fortunately, as the tide receded, 'Splash's' ordeal came to an end and he lived to fight another day.

'Waves' is one of the mums who has not read the seal rule book. She has pups that seem to prefer spending time in the water from an early age and she has now had 7 pups at 3 different sites 75km apart within her range which goes all the way from east of Boscastle on the north coast to Looe in southeast Cornwall. This represents a minimum straight line, headland to headland distance of 225km.

Seals love playing with seaweed and lost fishing net presents a similar pleasure sometimes with dire consequences. I have watched a seal called 'Pacific' play with a raft of trawl net, lying on it like a mattress at the surface and tipping himself off before realising a flipper is caught. A seal's panic response is to spin and this can be fatal on a trawl net mattress or pot line.

During numerous beach cleans, fishing gear and storm damaged or lost net are the main materials collected. Most seals become entangled whilst swimming up to and playing in and around floating rafts of lost net. Over 100 different live seals have been photo identified each year since 2016 in Cornwall and the Isles of Scilly with some form of entanglement – line, net, rope or hooked. The average live entanglement rate, compared to all seals observed at the West Cornwall site, has remained at 4% for 20 years with a maximum of 20 different live entangled seals seen on a single survey. In one month alone I have been distressed to have identified over 40 different entangled seals.

Most entanglement of live seals occurs in monofilament nets and around two thirds of injuries can be described as serious and potentially life threatening. Despite this, some seals survive a surprisingly long time with these horrific and presumably painful injuries. Our published research shows that many suffer for three years before dying, whilst the first live entangled seal I ever saw 'Lywans' has survived for 20 years despite her entanglement injuries. Small seals that become entangled are the most at risk, as they have a lot of growing to do into a net of fixed diameter. Juveniles tend to be easier to catch and immobilise, so rescue efforts are more practically focussed on relieving younger seals of their scarves or shawls of net.

Seals also die as a result of becoming entangled in long lengths of underwater net too heavy to drag to the surface. These seals asphyxiate as, being voluntary breathers, they simply don't inhale underwater. Rates of dead seal bycatch are currently not quantified, but a DEFRA report estimates 310 seals were dead bycaught around Devon and Cornwall in 2015 alone.

'Legs'

I first identified 'Legs' when she was a juvenile around three years old. A pretty, spotty girl frolicking in the shallows. Her story remained uneventful for six years when she delighted us all by having a pup under our noses on a mainland haul out beach. 'Leg's' pup was called 'Cliff' after the legendary singer, a favourite of our volunteer Tina Robinson, who inspired us all by setting up her own charity 'Our Only World'. 'Legs' was a great mum and her pup was massively fat and healthy when she left it at 3 weeks old. 'Legs' had to leave to feed herself after fasting throughout her lactation period to avoid herself from starving.

Four months later she was back, but this time with a very small amount of monofilament net trapped around her neck. If only we had been able to rescue her then, but circumstances did not allow. Within three weeks this loose noose had cut entirely through her skin all the way around her neck. Two years on, 'Legs' has a wound that can only be described as hideous. The net is now

A recent photo of 'Lucky Bunting'

embedded in her neck tissue with monofilament strands still blowing away from a big pink, raw wound with a strange ball of flesh visible at the top. Along with British Divers Marine Life Rescue and the Cornish Seal Sanctuary, we have plans to rescue her, but have not seen her at a time this has been possible from a human or seal safety perspective. This is a truly awful story to watch unfold and my heart hits my boots every time I see her and triage the rescue decision.

'Lucky Bunting'

Fortunately, not all entanglements are so heart breaking. I first met 'Lucky Bunting' in May 2016. She was a juvenile female sleeping peacefully amongst other wild seals on a remote haul out. By July, she had shocked me, when I realised it was her wearing a green trawl net shawl that was deeply, and presumably painfully, embedded in her neck. The following day I took part in a complex rescue that was successfully completed as I was able to cut the offending trawl net from her neck. A combined volunteer team from CSGRT and British Divers Marine Life Rescue celebrated as 'Lucky Bunting' rushed back to the safety of the sea.

I half expected never to see her back, thinking her experience here might have been so traumatic she would never return to the same beach. On the contrary, perhaps she realised this was where she suddenly felt better and free from her painful necklace, as within 30 days she was back resting peacefully again. I was genuinely surprised to discover that her deep and stinking wound was actually healing up well and by my next sighting, 55 days after her rescue, it had fully healed. How wonderful. Already a celebrity seal, 'Lucky Bunting's' story has got better ever since.

As a young adult, she taught us some new science...that females in their first season will attract multiple (in her case at least six) potential suiter males (not 'beachmasters') with whom she frolicked and cavorted for hours. Our volunteers photographed her mating with ten year old 'Three Scars' (boyfriend number five), not long before she left the site. When she returned a month later, 'Lucky Bunting' was no longer attracting or tolerating male company. Over the next few months, she continued to commute between her favourite haul out site and an offshore island monitored by a local boat operator. We never found out where 'Lucky Bunting' had her pup that year, but tracked her moving between her rescue, favourite onshore and offshore island sites for over 12 months.

Then we made the discovery we had all be waiting for! 'Lucky Bunting' did have a pup...and we knew where from day one! Sadly, it was at a very public site and we were worried that 'Lucky Bunting' would be too disturbed by the considerable clifftop footfall to feed her pup enough for it to stand any chance of survival. So, an ambitious plan was conceived with CSGRT and BDMLR volunteers teaming up for a 'round the clock' vigil. For 15 days during daylight hours, 36 different volunteers watched over 'Lucky Bunting' and her pup 'Little Flag'. We can't wait for the next chapter in 'Lucky Bunting's' lifestory!

Visitors didn't expect to see seals on their coastal walk past this site, many not knowing anything about grey seals, so were utterly amazed when they were told 'Lucky Bunting's' incredible tale by the amazing volunteer team. Individual seal stories like 'Lucky Bunting's' underpin the best kind of engagement we can do with the

Left to right: The disturbed seal looks at you...moves towards the water...enters the sea

public about seals. Seal stories connect people to the unknown world of grey seals and create emotional connections that last a lifetime. In the following 2 years 'Lucky Bunting' has successfully weaned 2 more pups.

Unlike many marine species, seals are exposed to a range of different anthropogenic effects when hauled out on land. In this respect, seals most resemble sea birds with their marine and terrestrial habitat requirements.

Disturbance is a complex issue dependent on the individual seal, prevailing wind conditions, the level of natural ambient sound from the wind and waves and the familiarity of the location to the seal. In the first instance, a seal's attention is likely to be attracted by hearing a sound (high pitched, excited voices or dog barks) or smelling something unfamiliar such as people. If a seal looks up and sees something unusual that is perceived as a threat, it is likely to move. If the danger stimulus disappears, the seal may resettle. If not, the seal is likely to return to the safety of the sea.

On land, seals become vulnerable to a wide range of human disturbance that affects their energy budget, compromising their nutritional state. Disturbing a hauled out seal reduces the amount of energy the seal can get from digesting its food, at the same time as using more energy to move into the sea and out again. So, disturbing a seal during its digestion break is like a double whammy to its energy budget. Repeated disturbance stampedes by humans can be as frequent as ten times in 70 minutes, emptying a haul out completely. This is likely to seriously compromise a seal's nutritional status. Most impacts of disturbance are invisible. Even a seal looking up and alert to your presence will have had their flight response activated. Adrenalin will be pumping, resulting in a raised heart and breathing rates (increasing energy expenditure). As a one-off this is not serious, but repeated visits by humans throughout a haul out day on the clifftop or by boats, results in chronic impacts similar to severe stress.

The best way to avoid disturbing seals is to be quiet, move slowly, keep a low profile and your distance and observe the seal's reactions to you. If it looks at you, it has been disturbed and you are too close. Any closer movement will result in the seal returning to the sea in a compromised state. General advice is that 100m is the minimum to approach a hauled out seal, which is a great range from which to observe seals through binoculars or a telescope. The three stages of disturbance are 1. the seal looks at you, 2. the seal moves towards the water, and 3. the seal enters the sea.

Any seal rushing towards the sea has been severely disturbed and photo ID shows

Pregnant female

that in most cases the seal swims away from the site and does not return to rest. During the moulting season with blood close to the surface of their skin, disturbance can increase heat loss and upset a seal's thermal balance. During the breeding season, the consequences of disturbance can be even more serious. A pregnant mother carries her pup in her lower abdomen. If disturbed, she may rush over sharp boulders to the safety of the sea, causing untold damage to her unborn pup. For all seals throughout the year disturbance can result in injury. Common injuries are gashed bellies and claws ripped out as they become trapped between boulders.

Close inspection after a stampede will show rocks covered with multiple blood trails. With a little knowledge and care, most seal disturbance can be avoided, leaving the seals to sleep in peace, for everyone to enjoy watching natural behaviour for longer. Seal disturbance is always a waste of energy, sometimes resulting in injury and may even prove fatal.

Seals that visit Cornwall's harbours face additional threats from the obvious, such as propeller wounds, to the less obvious of ingesting light grade diesel fuel oil, which if inhaled can lead to a slow shut down of key organs. Possibly the greatest risk to seals is our love of animals and desire to get close and interact with them. Feeding seals that are begging for food can lead them into a lifetime of humanised behaviour in a very dangerous environment. Feeding seals from and around boats, links boats and food in a seal's mind. During the winter, the only boats leaving the harbour are likely to be fishing boats around which seals are unwelcome visitors. Please learn from human experience with gulls, which are now considered a pest by some, and please never feed wild seals, however much they beg.

S326 'Box Desk'

"Horrifying and life changing" – that's one

Begging for food from a boat (left). Being fed mackerel (right)

person's description of the day their St Ives boat trip went badly wrong. As an enjoyable angling trip came to a close and the boat returned to St Ives harbour, customers gave in to the begging eyes of two seals – 'Box Desk' and 'Clouds' following their boat. Sadly, in a split second of unfortunate circumstances, adult female 'Box Desk' came up to grab a fish that had landed at the back of the boat at the same time as the skipper reversed to park quayside.

The sudden grating propeller sound meant 'Box Desk' had been seriously injured. It took onlookers a few moments to realise what had happened as the seal splashed vigorously at the surface and dashed away revealing a large pink injury that had nearly cut off her tail. 'Box Desk' disappeared completely for a month, presumably lying low to convalesce, giving her body a chance to heal. When she returned, we realised the severity of her injury, which was so nearly life threatening.

'Box Desk' must not be allowed to have suffered in vain. We are extremely lucky that her accident did not prove fatal for her, although we are still unclear about the fate of her unborn pup. We can all learn from this and make the lives of the seals in all harbours safer. The next time a seal looks longingly into your eyes, clearly begging for

food...be prepared, stay strong and say 'No!' We all need to pledge tough love and stop feeding seals – everywhere; now and forever!

Please 'Do not disturb' by Watching Seals Well: Key messages for watching seals

It is important for seals to rest on land, so we need to leave them there.
Avoid any activities near seals.
Never approach seals.

Disturbance is bad for a seal as it:
- Interrupts their rest
- Causes stress
- Wastes energy reserves
- Can result in injury or death

We have disturbed a seal if it is looking at us. Back away to avoid it moving. Seals injure themselves when we scare them into the sea.

Stay out of sight - seals close to shore may want to rest on land. We should not seek out encounters with seals in the sea. During a chance encounter we should keep moving. If seals make a big splash 'crash dive' it shows they are distressed.

We need to keep:
- Well away: use a camera's zoom, binoculars or telescope
- Dogs under control on leads
- Quiet (so seals can't hear us)
- Out of sight (so seals can't see us)
- Downwind (so seals can't smell us)
- Our litter with us by taking it home

Never:
- Get close (follow local advice)
- Fly drones near seals
- Feed a wild seal
- Scare seals or put pups into the sea
- Copy the bad behaviour of others
- Take a seal selfie
- Name seal sites online

Please follow advice on signs/fencing or from onsite volunteers.

Please avoid using photos of seals looking at the camera as this implies the seal has been disturbed. Good photos reflect natural wild behaviour with a seal oblivious to the photographer's presence. Good social media # include: #DoNotDisturb; #KeepYourDistance; #UseYourZoom; #GiveWildlifeSpace and #RespectTheNap.

SEALS AND PEOPLE

In 2000, it was just me with my growing interest in seals. I took my first seal record that year and set up Cornwall Seal Group in 2004 with friends I had met on the clifftops. By 2008 we had begun to expand our network further afield, our work dictated by the movements of the seals. In 2015 we registered as a charity 'Cornwall Seal Group Research Trust' (No. 1162936). Two years later we had our first 'Amazement and Discovery' Ranger and now we have four more Marine Rangers – 'Research', 'Creativity and Activity', 'Sanctuaries at Sea' and 'Digital'.

Most importantly our Marine Rangers have set up and support a network of 25 voluntary, community-based Photo ID teams. These hubs monitor, research, ID, protect and represent their local seals and the marine habitat they need. As CSGRT celebrated its 20th birthday, our charity has expanded from one to over 450 amazing and inspiring volunteers, led by our Patron Gillian Burke, the Springwatch presenter. We are all dedicated to ensuring Cornwall's grey seals thrive for future generations to enjoy.

A rescued seal, 'Myrtle' (left), and the net that was removed from around her neck (right)

How did this happen? Well, we were always serious seal recorders, but our top aim has always been to have fun and this is as true today as it was back then. If people don't enjoy watching and recording seals, they soon stop and seals need people for the long term. People often think we 'do' seals, but actually most of our work is with people! Seals are far too busy enjoying themselves to be bothered by what we are up to. Yet sadly their fate is in our hands. Seals need people and local ambassadors to look out for them and to champion their cause.

We now represent seals at a national level, chairing the 'Seal Alliance' disturbance working group, inputting evidence to DEFRA's Seal Network UK and as members of DEFRA's 'Clean Catch UK' National Steering Group. CSGRT work with four global organisations – World Animal Protection, the Global Ghost Gear Initiative, the Pinniped Entanglement Group and the 5 Gyres Trawlshare microplastics project. Marine issues require global solutions and seals need a voice representing them if their future conservation is to be effective.

Partnership working is critical to share our combined skill sets and expand our influence and impact. Our first and closest partners were British Divers Marine Life Rescue, the Cornish Seal Sanctuary and the RSPCA Wildlife Centre at West Hatch.

This seal rescue summarises one example of how we collaborate with partners to find consensus in a world that is far from clear cut. Routine survey work can turn out to be anything other than routine, if one of the seals on the haul out turns out to be a 6 month old seal entangled in monofilament net. Rescue decisions are tough and full of grey areas. So many factors must be considered before taking the decision to rescue a seal and the safety of the rescuers is paramount.

Not all entangled seals observed can be rescued but, like 'Lucky Bunting', one of the fortunate ones was 'Myrtle'. All rescues are co-ordinated by British Divers Marine Life Rescue in collaboration with the Cornish Seal Sanctuary at Gweek or, if they are full, the RSPCA Wildlife Centre at West Hatch. The tide was coming in and the seal's position meant a rescue needed to be swift to stand any chance of success. Access to remote beaches can be hazardous and for 'Myrtle's' rescue a rope safety team of two was needed. After scaling the precipitous slopes, the seal rescue team of three made it to the beach without being spotted by 'Myrtle' – had she heard or seen them, she would have bolted for the sea and all the rescuers' efforts

would have been in vain. Using the cover of rocks for as long as possible, the two most experienced seal handlers, Dan and Tim, made their way across the open beach in a crouched position until 'Myrtle' finally lifted her head and spotted them.

In no time at all 'Myrtle' had turned around and shot off for the sea. Had she not had a split second's indecision about which of two routes to take, she would have escaped, but her slight delay gave Dan and Tim the time they needed to spring into action, sprinting towards the seal and catching her in the shallows. Dan launched himself at 'Myrtle' and as Tim and Rob arrived, they were able to immobilise her and take her to drier land. After assessing 'Myrtle's' wounds, they removed the net tightly encircling her neck, but her deep wounds needed treatment, so the decision was made to take her to the Cornish Seal Sanctuary at Gweek.

Hauling any seal up the cliff is tough work and 'Myrtle' weighed in at a hefty 31.5 kilos, taking the strength of all five rescuers to get her to the cliff top. The experienced Animal Care Team at Gweek are used to nursing seals with this type of injury back to health, so in just three short weeks 'Myrtle' was healed and ready to return to the wild and just over a month later she was spotted fit, well and fat back at the wild seal haul out having been given a second chance, doing all the things that normal seals do – chasing around, playing and having fun!

Nearly all seals that have been rehabilitated at one of the many seal rescue centres around the UK are given a coloured rear flipper tag with a unique reference number. Virtually all the seals being cared for at Gweek have been rescued in Cornwall and are released back in Cornish waters. Overflow seals rescued in Cornwall go to West Hatch and are released in north Devon. Reporting any tags that you see, their colour, which side flipper they were on and the reference number really helps add to our understanding of the life and times of grey seals. Frequently, rehabilitated seals are accused of hanging around in harbours and fishing nets, but this is a myth, as only two tagged seals in 20 years have ever actually been observed doing this.

The rescue of 'Myrtle'

What to do if you see...

A white coated seal pup, that is likely to be dependent on its mother:

- Please keep away and always avoid being smelt/seen or heard by a pup and its mum
- Watch onshore/offshore for pup/mum for 30 minutes
- NEVER go near a seal pup
- NEVER put a seal pup back in the sea

- Ring British Divers Marine Life Rescue on their 24 hour hotline 01825 765546 if you are concerned. Trained medics or staff will be dispatched to your location as soon as possible.

An entangled, injured, visibly thin or unwell seal of any age:

Please remember that if you scare this seal into the sea, rescuers are unlikely to be able to capture or help it. Please ring the British Divers Marine Life Rescue on their 24 hotline 01825 765546 and again retreat to a safe distance from where you can observe the seal from a place where you can't be smelt, heard or seen.

A dead seal:

We can probably learn as much, if not more, about live seals from dead seals! Please call the Cornwall Wildlife Trust's Marine Strandings Network on 0345 201 26 26 and they will send out trained volunteers to take photos along with detailed measurements and records about the seal. Whilst there is currently limited funding for seal post mortems, a few are done each year on cases where the cause of death is unclear.

Photo identification research findings

Detailed surveys and photo identification by our incredible volunteer network and partner organisations have been carried out since 2000 at sites around the southwest from south Wales and Somerset, via the Isles of Scilly to Dorset. Seals from this area have been linked up to Wales, Ireland, France, Belgium and Holland. Who knew seals in Cornwall were so well travelled?

Individual seal life histories and calendars reveal a huge variation in individual behaviour. Established haul out sites do not appear to be discrete colonies of seals, but rather service stations on seal motorways.

Less than a handful of seals have been recorded spending the entire year at a single site, with most seals appearing to have their

If we have learned anything about Cornwall's grey seals, it is that (as with humans) there is no such thing as an average seal. There is so much more for us to learn and by collaborating with a wide range of organisations we learn the most. Come and join our movement...you don't have to live in Cornwall to help us learn more about seals in Cornwall! Please email your seal records, photos and volunteer offers to sightings@cornwallsealgroup.co.uk

'Canvey'

Rescued in 1996 and rehabilitated at the Cornish Seal Sanctuary at Gweek, 'Canvey' was released back into the wild a few months later. Between 2000 and February 2006, 'Canvey' was seen just once a year at the West Cornwall site, despite being an easily recognisable seal. In September 2006, at the age of 10, 'Canvey' was recorded dead in Porthleven. From cradle to grave, 'Canvey' had been monitored, yet we still know so little about where he spent the bulk of his life and whilst his death provided closure, it posed more questions than it provided answers! 'Canvey' was my original driving force. I wanted to fill in gaps in the stories of his friends and tell the world more about these amazing, globally rare marine creatures.

own personal combination of moulting, breeding and offshore foraging site in any twelve month period.

Each offshore foraging site may have a small number of regular visitors for six or seven months of the year, whilst the larger mainland haul out sites are mostly frequented by migrants during their swim around the coast between their other favourite places. Some individual seals visit vast ranges of coastal habitat (such as 'Tulip Belle') whilst others have mostly only ever been recorded at a single site (pretty much like 'Chairlift') and some just completely disappear from our radar for much of the year (like 'Ghost').

I have found my niche in life, I love grey seals, am passionate about them - this is what I am here for! Someone has to do this work and help to provide a voice for grey seals in a natural world shaped by humans and the daily decisions we all make.

Synopsis

Cornwall's most iconic marine mammal is also its most reliable and frequently spotted, despite grey seals being one of the rarest seal species in the world. Cornish grey seals are part of a genetically distinct sub population that is globally significant. It is our international, moral and legal obligation to protect grey seals, yet there is much still to be discovered about this charismatic species.

About the author

Sue Sayer has lived in Cornwall since 1991. She has spent thousands of hours remotely observing grey seals in the wild, which has given her an unparalleled insight into the behaviour of these curious and playful marine creatures. Able to recognise individual seals by sight, their appearance on a Cornish beach after a long absence is like the return of an old friend. In 2004, Sue set up Cornwall Seal Group (now Cornwall Seal Group Research Trust aka Seal Research Trust), which has a healthy, active network of incredible and inspiring citizen scientists, who meet once a month. In 2008, Sue gave up her day job to study seals full time. She has volunteered for the charity ever since, trying to make a lasting difference for grey seals everywhere, by sharing her passion and knowledge with anyone who will listen!

How Sue would like seals to look – relaxed and snoozy

Resources

A wide variety of Seal Research Trust public resources are available to download:

https://drive.google.com/drive/folders/1tB4_XeUtQ4a-hx5FYT0GMrOC4f5HebQSr?usp=sharing

This contains
- Advice on best practice for different coastal users
- Recording forms and risk assessments
- Graphics for social media, signs and leaflets
- Key messages
- Reference resources
- Reference reports
- Rescues

Useful organisations

British Divers Marine Life Rescue (to report injured or distressed seals you are concerned about)
01825 765546 : http://www.bdmlr.org.uk/

Cornwall Seal Group Research Trust (aka Seal Research Trust)
- sightings@cornwallsealgroup.co.uk (to report live seal sightings)
- seals@cornwallsealgroup.co.uk (to access free remote 'on demand', online volunteer training)
- www.cornwallsealgroup.co.uk and www.sealresearchtrust.com
- https://www.youtube.com/@cornwallsealgroupresearchtrust/videos
- https://www.facebook.com/CornwallSealGroupResearchTrust/
- https://www.instagram.com/cornwallsealgroupresearchtrust/
- https://twitter.com/cornwallsealGRT
- https://www.linkedin.com/in/sue-sayer-917b3a2a

Cornwall Wildlife Trust 01872 272939
https://www.cornwallwildlifetrust.org.uk/

Cornwall Marine and Coastal Code
(to report seal disturbance) 0345 201 26 26
https://cornwallmarinelifecode.org.uk/

Cornwall Wildlife Trust's Marine Strandings Network
(to report dead marine life of any kind in Cornwall)
0345 201 26 26 https://www.cornwallwildlifetrust.org.uk/what-we-doour-conservation-workat-sea/marine-strandings-network https://www.cornwallwildlifetrust.org.uk/what-we-do/our-conservation-work/at-sea/marine-strandings-network

The Cornish Seal Sanctuary 01326 221361
https://www.sealsanctuary.co.uk/corn1.html

Seal Alliance : http://www.sealalliance.org/

Tara Seal Research Centre http://www.sealresearch.org/

Cetacean Strandings Investigation Programme
(to report dead marine life of any kind elsewhere in the UK) 0800 6520333 http://ukstrandings.org/

The National Trust http://www.nationaltrust.org.uk/

RSPCA West Hatch Wildlife Centre 0300 1234999
https://www.facebook.com/RSPCAWesthatchwildlife

Sea Mammal Research Unit
UK seals ID http://www.smru.st-andrews.ac.uk/files/2016/08/Identifying-Seals-Leaflet.pdf : Seal diet http://www.smru.st-andrews.ac.uk/files/2016/08/Seal-Diet-Leaflet.pdf

South West Marine Ecosystems
http://swmecosystems.co.uk/

- Annual seal webinars https://www.youtube.com/watch?v=ZTSPkDkyhsY and https://www.youtube.com/watch?v=ZTSPkDkyhsY
- Annual seal reports https://swmecosystems.co.uk/annual-reports

Wildlife Safe Scheme (National training for minimising disturbance to marine wildlife) https://www.wisescheme.org/

Interesting seal books
Sheila Anderson: Seals by Whittet, 1990
Sheila Anderson: The Grey Seal by Shire Natural History, 1988
W Nigel Bonner: The Natural History of Seals by Christopher Helm, 1989
Susan Richardson: Where the Seals Sing by William Collins, 2022
Paul Thompson: The Common Seal by Shire Natural History, 1989

Stephen Westcott: The Grey Seals of the West Country by CWT, 1997

A selection of children's books are available from https://www.sealresearchtrust.com/collections

Publications and reports
Entanglement of grey seals at a haul out site in Cornwall, UK. Allen, R., Jarvis, D., Sayer, S. & Mills, C. by Marine Pollution Bulletin, 2012
Monitoring grey seal pupping sites in Cornwall 2016. Sayer, S., & Witt, M.J., Natural England, 2017

Pinnipeds, people and photo-identification: the implications of grey seal movements for effective management of the species. Sayer, S., Allen, R., Hawkes, L.A., Hockley, K., Jarvis, D., & Witt, M.J., Journal of the Marine Biological Association, 2019

Post release monitoring of rehabilitated grey seal pups over large temporal and spatial scales. Sayer, S., Allen, R., Bellman, K., Beaulieu, M., Cooper, T., Dyer, N., Hockin, K., Hockley, K., Jarvis, D., Jones, G., Oaten, P., Waddington, N., Witt, M.J., Hawkes, L., Marine Mammal Science, 2021

'Willow' the moulted seal pup who can now be ID'd for life by CSGRT (left). Just like 'Chairlift' – Sue's first ID in 2000 still thriving in 2022 (right)